Academic phrase

A lot of...	Many, numerous, a l considerable amount/quantity
More and more...	Increasingly
I thought at first that it would be good...	It seemed initially a good solution
So I changed this word for another word...	Consequently/therefore I replaced the word with another lexical item
But I thought that this wouldn't be a good thing to do...	I did not, however, appear to be a good choice/solution
I am sure that these two are similar...	There seems to be a definite resemblance between the two ...
I reckon, I consider, I think, I believe, in my opinion... I don't think... I am not sure...	It appears, it seems, it is likely that... it is unlikely that... it is not certain whether....
... but I was not sure if I made the right decision ...	However, I was not convinced that my original decision was correct...
Later I thought that perhaps I did not use the best way to use ...	It occurred to me that it might not have been the best procedure to employ ...
Use, employ, apply	
Advantage, benefit	
Challenge, difficulty, problem, issue	
Apparently, seemingly, ostensibly	
Method, technique, strategy, procedure	
Relevance, importance, significance, pertinence	
Help, assist, aid, contribute, improve	
Using this method did not bring the result that I expected to achieve	Employing this procedure failed to produce the expected result

Newmark, P. (1988) A textbook of translation

Baker 2011

Delisle Jean et al, ed. (1999) Translation Terminology
Amsterdam and Philadelphia: John
Benjamins

Belcuyk

Baker   Hatim & Mason 1980

Fawcett   Halliday 2 Hasen
                                                    1976

Stronki od p. Am   Nida and Tabor 1974

Wikipedia

PWN Oxford dictionary

Słownik medyczny

TASK ONE

Refer to the following Teaching Tips.

Teaching Tips

Useful Phrases

Comparing and contrasting	Both of these ...
	Neither of these ...
	One of these ..., while the other ...
	This one ..., but on the other hand that one ...
Speculating	It seems to me that ...
	It's hard to say, but I think ...
	It looks like a ...
	I'd say ...
	It must be ...
	It might be ...
	It could be ...
	It can't be ...
	I don't think it ..., because ...
Expressing opinions	Personally speaking ...
	Speaking personally ...
	Personally, I ...
	I've never thought about it, but I suppose ...
	I don't really like ..., but if I had to choose ...
	It's very difficult to say, but I think ...

Practise Part 2 with your students. This will enable them to approach this part of the test with more confidence in the examination.

SUPPLEMENTARY TASK

TASK ONE *vague*

This will depend on the student's answers. Teachers can add their own suggestions.

abstracting

Teaching Tips

Useful Phrases

Initiating/focusing

So we have to ...
There are several possibilities for ...
Let's talk about ...first, shall we?
Let's see what the good points are, shall we?
I think they/we will/would need to ...
We have to choose ...
We have to decide which ...

Opinions/views/ideas

I think ...
What do you think ...
From what I know ...
In my opinion ...
As far as I'm concerned ...
Personally speaking ...
Could I just add that ...
If I might come in here ...
Don't you think ...
I've heard ...
I'm sure ...

Agreeing

That's a good point.
I couldn't have put it better myself.
I couldn't agree more.
I'm sure you're right.
I hadn't thought of that.
What a good idea!
Really.
Exactly!

Disagreeing

I see what you mean, but don't you think ...
Yes, but isn't it true that ...
I'm sure that's wrong.

Handwritten annotations:

It looks like *some kind of type* ....
yellowy thing with a sort of blue-ish shadow

There is a kind of machine or sth

It looks a bit like A. Lincoln

I can't quite figure/make it out, but it ...

I can't picture it in my head

If you look at it from a distance / closely / close up ... ... you can see ...

When I look at this → I feel ...
It makes me
reminds me

I can't quite put my finger
• why I think it's effective
• why I don't like it
• why I really love it, But ...

I'm not entirely sure what ? about this ...
→ whether this is effective as ad campaign

C Here is the final paragraph of the story. Some of the words that contribute to the cohesion have been left blank. What are they? Write one word in each blank.

Sadly, (1)_____ the morning, the nurse found Mick dead, (2)_____ she reassured Keith that he would soon have some more company. (3)_____ hearing this, Keith was quick to insist that it was his turn to have the bed by the window. (4)_____ first, the nurses tried to tell him why it would be easier if he stayed where he was, but he became (5)_____ angry that they finally carried him across to the other bed. He lay still for a while, waiting to be alone. Then, as (6)_____ as the nurses had gone, he lifted himself up expectantly (7)_____ peered through the window – to see a solid brick wall.

B Linking words

1.0 Conjunctions and sentence adverbials

A conjunction connects two clauses in the same sentence. (A clause is a phrase with a verb in it.)

*I have been watching television **since** I got home at six o'clock.*

A sentence adverb (or adverbial phrase)

- can connect a sentence with another sentence.
  *I got home at six o'clock. **Since then**, I have been watching television.*

- can connect a sentence with the whole text.
  *. . . and then I went to bed. **All in all**, I had a very boring evening.*

- can signal the writer's attitude to what they are saying.
  Frankly, *I wish I didn't have a television.*
  To be honest

The lists on pages 21 and 23 group these words according to their function (for example, to indicate a relationship of time). Note that a few conjunctions can also be used as sentence adverbials. But note also that the practice of beginning a sentence with *and*, *but* or *or*, though common today – even among good writers – is often thought incorrect.

A These sentences focus on the distinction between conjunctions, in the *a* sentences, and sentence adverbials. Using the lists on page 23, fill the gaps in the *b* sentences with a sentence adverbial, so that the two sentences have the same meaning. The first has been done as an example.

Time
1a (conj) Silvia went for a swim *after* she had done her homework
1b (adv) Silvia did her homework. *Afterwards*, she went for a swim.

2a She was dying for a swim *by the time* she had finished studying.
2b She studied till midday. By then, she was dying for a swim.

3a *While* she was swimming, I continued to study.
3b I continued to study. Meanwhile, she was swimming.

Reason and result
4a The Addams live in a strange house, *so* they don't get many visitors.
4b The Addams live in a strange house. Because of this, they don't get many visitors.

5a *Since* she had promised to visit him, she went there the next day.
5b She had promised to visit him. For this reason she went there the next day.

Contrast and concession
6a A lot of men are uncomfortable with Morticia, *even though* she has a sweet nature.
6b Morticia has a sweet nature. _____, a lot of men are uncomfortable with her.

7a The English eat potatoes, *whereas* the Chinese eat rice.
7b The English eat potatoes. The Chinese, _____, eat rice.

Addition
8a *Not only* does Marcel play the trumpet, *but* he can *also* juggle.
8b Marcel plays the trumpet. _____, he can juggle.

B Conjunctions (and prepositions)

Most of the words in this table are conjunctions and join two clauses. The words marked (P), however, are prepositions, and are followed by either a noun or a gerund (-ing form).

Time	Contrast, Concession, Alternatives		if	much as
after+		just in case	on condition that	the way
after which	**Concession,**	on account of (P)	provided (that)	
and	**Alternatives**	seeing as / that	providing (that)	**Addition**
as	although	since	so long as	and+
as long as	apart from (P)		unless	as well as (P)
as soon as	but	**Purpose**	whether . . . or	besides (P)
at which (point)	despite (P)	in case		besides which
before+	even if	in order that	**Manner**	in addition to (P)
by the time	even though	in order to	as	not only*
hardly*	except that	so	as if	
no sooner*	in spite of (P)	so as to	as though	**Giving examples**
now (that)	or	so that	in a way	for instance (P)
once	much as	to	in the way	for example (P)
since	nor		just as	in particular (P)
the moment	not that	**Conditional**	like	
then	though	as long as		
till+	whereas	even if		
until+	while			
when	whilst			
whenever	yet			
whereupon				
while	**Reason**			
	as			
Result	as a result of (P)			
and	because			
and so	because of (P)			
else	considering			
or else	due to			
otherwise	for			
so	in case			
so that	in view of the fact that			

* Inversion – note the word order after these words when they begin the sentence.

We had hardly left the ground *when* the storm broke.
Hardly **had we** left the ground *when* the storm broke.

The plane had no sooner taken off *than* I regretted not taking the train.
No sooner **had the plane** taken off *than* I regretted not taking the train.

+ These words can act as either prepositions or conjunctions.
He went to bed **after** *midnight.* (preposition)
He went to bed **after** *he had finished his book.* (conjunction)

The sentences below illustrate many of the linking words in the table. Note that many conjunctions can be used either in the middle of a sentence

I wouldn't have told the police **even if** I had known. (sentences 1–9)

or at the beginning.

Even if I had known, I wouldn't have told the police. (sentences 10–12)

Complete the sentences by adding any appropriate word or phrase: note which conjunctions are used with commas in the examples.

1 We are advised to do this exercise very
   a carefully, *otherwise* we will make a lot of _mistakes_ .
   b carefully(,) *while* our teacher _is watching -us_ .
   c carefully, *even though* it looks _easy_ .

2 My weeks in captivity weren't too
   a unpleasant(,) *considering* the terrible reputation of _kiddnapers_
   b unpleasant *once* I got used to _conditions_ .
   c unpleasant, *even if* the _food/situation_ was terrible.

3 The tigers ran away from the
   a Englishwoman *as if* she _was a monster_
   b Englishwoman *the way* _they would_ run away from _monster_ .
   c Englishwoman *the moment* they saw _her_ .

4 Her Olympic gold medal was
   a remarkable, *though* many people _____ .
   b remarkable, *not that* she didn't deserve _it /how_
   c remarkable *in view of the fact that* she had just _recovered_ .

Oxford Practice Grammar

Intermediate

Lesson plans and worksheets

Rachel Godfrey

OXFORD
UNIVERSITY PRESS

OXFORD
UNIVERSITY PRESS

Great Clarendon Street, Oxford OX2 6DP

Oxford University Press is a department of the University of Oxford.
It furthers the University's objective of excellence in research, scholarship,
and education by publishing worldwide in

Oxford New York

Auckland Cape Town Dar es Salaam Hong Kong Karachi
Kuala Lumpur Madrid Melbourne Mexico City Nairobi
New Delhi Shanghai Taipei Toronto

With offices in

Argentina Austria Brazil Chile Czech Republic France Greece
Guatemala Hungary Italy Japan Poland Portugal Singapore
South Korea Switzerland Thailand Turkey Ukraine Vietnam

OXFORD and OXFORD ENGLISH are registered trade marks of
Oxford University Press in the UK and in certain other countries

Any websites referred to in this publication are in the public domain and
their addresses are provided by Oxford University Press for information only.
Oxford University Press disclaims any responsibility for the content

ISBN: 978 0 19 457989 6

Printed in China

Contents

Introduction

These lesson plans have been prepared as a resource for teachers, to accompany classroom use of the *Oxford Practice Grammar* series. There are 22 lessons, each based on a particular unit in the book.

How the lesson plans work

Alongside the detailed grammar information and controlled written practice activities provided in the book, the plans provide these lesson components:

- a **demonstration** stage to show the language points in context and use
- suggestions for teacher-led **clarification**, including concept-check questions, form-check questions, timelines and other board-based ideas for making meaning and form clear
- **extra activities** whose purpose is to give additional 'heads-up' practice of an aspect of the grammar point, and to change the pace and energy of the lesson. Some of these are very controlled practice activities: whole-class oral drills, including transformation drills, cue/response drills and substitution drills, as well as open-pair (or 'across the class') activities. Others are short games or speaking activities.
- extended, **freer speaking and writing practice** activities to activate the language that has been clarified.

About the worksheets

Every lesson plan includes a photocopiable worksheet. The worksheets are interactive, calling for pair work, group work or a combination of both.

Most of the worksheets are used towards the end of the lesson as the basis of a final communicative speaking or writing activity. Many of them allow the students to personalize the language they have just studied.

Some of the worksheets are adaptations of the exercises in the book, so that an interactive element is brought to the controlled practice stage of the lesson.

In a very few cases (mainly in the Intermediate book), the worksheet is used at the demonstration/clarification stage to informally test the students' knowledge of the grammar point.

'At a glance'

Each lesson plan begins with an 'At a glance' section, providing a summary overview of the lesson. It shows the lesson aims and objectives, and gives a guideline to the staging of the lesson, the use of the worksheet, and the final lesson outcome.

It shows which grammar points from the book unit are focused on in the lesson (in some cases the lesson covers all the points in a unit, in others it only focuses on one or two).

Preparation

The lessons are designed to be prepared quickly and easily. For some lessons, flashcards and pictures need to be prepared in advance for the clarification and/or demonstration stages. Some of the extra activities require prompts on the board: these can be copied on to an OHT (overhead transparency) if an OHP (overhead projector) is available to the teacher.

1 Unit 3 Direct and indirect objects

At a glance

1 This lesson clarifies these structures with **direct and indirect objects**:
- Structure 1: verb + indirect object + direct object
- Structure 2: verb + direct object + **to/for** + indirect object
- Structure 3: verb + object pronoun + direct object.

2 The lesson also focuses on a number of verbs which take **to** (e.g. **give, read, sell, show**)

and some others which take **for** (e.g. **choose, reserve, cook, make**).

3 **Exercises A** and **B** in the book give controlled written practice in Structures 1 and 2. **Exercise C** focuses on **to** and **for**, and **Exercise D** gives practice in Structure 3.

4 The **worksheet 'You, people and things'** provides the students with an opportunity for freer, personalized practice of the language in the form of a questionnaire and discussion.

Lesson length

45–60 minutes

Preparation

- Copy the five pictures (the watch, the sweater, the scarf, the tennis racquet, and the necklace) from Exercise A on to cards (about A4 size).
- You will need Blu-tack or a similar adhesive to stick these pictures to the board.
- Photocopy one worksheet for each student in the class.

Demonstration 1

1 Show the cards (the watch, the sweater, the scarf, the tennis racquet, and the necklace) to the class and make sure they can name all the items.

2 Give the cards to different students in the class. Ask those students to give their own item to someone else in the class.

3 Now, using your students' names, write on the board the beginnings of sentences about what happened. For example:

> Rafael gave …
> Minna gave …

4 Elicit from the students two different ways to complete the sentences and write them on the board:

> Rafael gave Kiki a watch.   Rafael gave a watch to Kiki.
> Minna gave Samuel a sweater.   Minna gave a sweater to Samuel.

Clarification 1

Give + two objects – Structure 1 and Structure 2 (1)

1 To focus on the structure of the sentences, ask the class: *What or who is the subject of each sentence?* [Rafael.] *What or who is the direct object of the sentence?* [A watch.] *What or who is the indirect object of the sentence?* [Kiki.] Highlight the structure on the board:

Structure 1		
subject	indirect object	direct object
Rafael gave	Kiki	a watch.
Structure 2		
subject	direct object	indirect object
Rafael gave	a watch	to Kiki.

2 Point out that there is no **to** in Structure 1.

3 Students may feel more comfortable using Structure 2. Explain that it is more usual to hear and use Structure 1 in English.

4 Ask students to suggest other verbs like **give** that can have two objects in the sentence [**send, write, lend**].

Practice 1

Exercise A (individuals)

- Ask your students to do Exercise A. Make sure they all use Structure 1.
- When checking the answers with the whole class, make sure the students stress the key words in the sentence, e.g. *Harriet gave Mike a watch*.

Exercise B (individuals)

- Ask your students to do Exercise B. In this case students sometimes need to use Structure 1, sometimes Structure 2. Do the two examples with the class to show this.
- When checking the answers, you could ask the students to say the alternative structure in each case, e.g. *Mark sent a message to his boss. Mark sent his boss a message.*

Exercise B Extension activity (pairs)

- Once the students have completed Exercise B and you have checked the answers with the whole class, students can test each other with this extension activity.
- Student A closes her/his book. Student B reads out the first sentence of each pair of sentences in the exercise (e.g. *Emma sold her bike.*) Student A must then try to remember and produce the longer sentence (*Emma sold her bike to her sister.*)
- The pairs then swap roles, so Student B closes his/her book and is tested by Student A.

Demonstration 2

1 Stick the picture of the scarf to the board. Ask the students: *What else can you do with a scarf?* Mime actions to elicit some verbs from the class [e.g. **make**, **lend**, **send**, **show**, **choose**].

2 Write two example sentences on the board. For example:

> I made a scarf for Anita.
> I showed the scarf to Carmen.

Clarification 2

To or for? (2)

1 Tell students that these verbs can also be used in the two structures already seen in the lesson, e.g. *I made a scarf for Anita. I made Anita a scarf.*

2 Explain that in Structure 2, some of the verbs take **to**, others take **for**. Write the verbs from the demonstration in two columns on the board. Ask the students if they can add any more to the lists.

to	for
lend	make
send	choose
post	
show	

Direct the students to Section 2 on page 6 to see other verbs with two objects that take **to** and **for**.

Practice 2

Exercise C (individuals)

- Ask your students to do Exercise C. Ask them to check their answers in pairs before you check the answers together as a class.

Exercise C Extra activity (teams)

- Tell the students to close their books. Write this table on the board:

send	a table	to Jim
offer	a letter	for Jim
book	a book	
lend	a postcard	
make	some money	
show	an ice cream	
fetch	a file	
write	a memo	
	a coffee	

- Divide the students into teams. The teams take it in turns to make sentences using the words in the table in a logical and grammatically correct way, e.g. *I sent a postcard to Jim.*
- Words can be used more than once, but each sentence must be different.
- Record the teams' correct sentences on the board. The team with the greatest number of correct sentences wins.

Clarification 3

Give + pronoun (3)

1 Tell students to look at Exercise A in their books again. Say: *What did Harriet give Mike? ~ She … to* elicit the answer: *She gave him a watch.*

Write on the board:

> She gave <u>him</u> a watch.

and underline 'him'.

2 Tell students that when a pronoun is used for the indirect object, Structure 1 is used:

> Structure 1
> subject indirect object direct object
> She gave him   a watch.
> (Not ~~She gave a watch to him.~~)

3 Tell students that when both the objects are pronouns, Structure 2 is used:

Structure 2			
subject		direct object	indirect object
She	gave	it	to him.
(Not ~~She gave him it.~~)			

Practice 3

Extra activity (whole class)
QUESTION AND ANSWER DRILL

- Give the class very controlled oral practice of **give** + pronoun with this drill. Ask questions about the people and objects in Exercise A in the book. The students must use pronouns for the subject and indirect object in their answers, not names.

  T: What did Harriet give Mike?
  SS: She gave him a watch.

  T: What did David give Melanie?
  SS: He gave her a sweater.

  T: What did Laura give Trevor?
  SS: She gave him a scarf.

  T: What did Emma give Matthew?
  SS: She gave him a tennis racquet.

  T: What did Henry give Claire?
  SS: He gave her a necklace.

- Go through the drill a few times until the students are producing the sentences comfortably.

Exercise D (pairs)

- Put the students in pairs and give them five to ten minutes to complete Exercise D. When checking the answers, you could ask the class to suggest alternative endings to the sentences, e.g. *What are you doing with those bottles? ~ I'm taking them to a party.*

Extra activity Worksheet (groups)
YOU, PEOPLE AND THINGS

- Give each student a copy of the worksheet questionnaire. Go through the first two questions yourself as examples.
- Give the students five to ten minutes to read and complete the questionnaire. As they are completing it, go round the class to check that they are filling in the 'things' and 'people' shapes correctly.
- Put the students into small groups to compare and discuss their answers. After about ten minutes invite the groups to report back on what they have learned about each other.

Lesson 1 Worksheet

You, people and things

1 For each question, tick ✓the answer that is true for you. Write the names of people and things in the shapes.

[a thing]   (a person)

1 Have you ever given flowers to anyone?

   A I've given (   ) flowers. [   ]

   B I've never given anyone flowers. [   ]

2 Do you owe anyone money at the moment?

   A I owe (   ) some money. [   ]

   B I don't owe anyone anything. [   ]

3 Are you going to send an email or text message today?

   A I'm going to send (   ) [   ] [   ]

   B I'm not going to send anyone an email or text message. [   ]

4 Have you ever chosen a book, CD, or clothes for someone else?

   A I once chose [   ] for (   ). [   ]

   B I've never chosen anything for anyone. [   ]

5 Have you ever made a card or present for anyone?

   A I once made (   ) [   ] [   ]

   B I've never made anything for anyone. [   ]

6 Have you ever sold anything to anyone?

   A I once sold [   ] to (   ). [   ]

   B I've never sold anything to anyone. [   ]

7 Do you write letters to anyone?

   A I sometimes write letters to (   ). [   ]

   B I never write letters to anyone. [   ]

8 Have you ever cooked a meal for more than two people?

   A I once cooked [   ] for (   ). [   ]

   B I've never cooked for more than two people. [   ]

   C I've never cooked anything for anyone. [   ]

2 Work in groups. Compare and discuss your answers.

2 Unit 6 Present Continuous or Present Simple?

At a glance

1 This lesson reviews and contrasts:
- the **Present Continuous** to talk about things happening now, and to talk about situations that we see as temporary
- the **Present Simple** to talk about repeated actions, thoughts, feelings, states, facts and situations that we see as permanent.

2 The **worksheet 'Where's Neil?'** is an adaptation of **Exercise A** in the book, and contrasts some of the uses of these two tenses in a pair-work gap-fill activity.

3 The **extension activity 'Changing the facts'** gives the students freer practice of these uses of the tenses within the same context as the worksheet.

4 **Exercise B** in the book gives controlled written practice of all of the uses of the Present Simple and Present Continuous focused on in the lesson.

5 The **extra activity 'It's a hard life'** provides the students with an opportunity for freer, personalized spoken practice.

Lesson length

45–60 minutes

Preparation

- Photocopy one worksheet for each pair of students. Cut the worksheets in half.
- Copy the sentences for the demonstrations and for the extra activity 'It's a hard life' on to an OHT if you plan to use the OHP.

Demonstration 1

1 As a warm-up, ask students to call out different places where people work. Write their answers on the board, for example:

> in an office   in a school   at home
> outdoors   in a shop   in a factory
> underground   at an airport   at a prison
> at a café or restaurant

2 Find out who in the class works/studies (or has worked/studied) in any of these environments.

3 Write these sentences on the board or project them on an OHP. Put the students in pairs for a few minutes to complete them, using the verb in brackets:

> 1 I can't talk now. I _____ (work).
> 2 I _____ (work) in a café at the weekends.
> 3 I _____ (think) your job is very interesting.
> 4 I _____ (think) about finding a new job.
> 5 The machines at the factory _____ (make) a lot of noise.
> 6 I'm busy at the moment. I _____ (make) sandwiches.

Check the answers with the whole class and write them on the board:

> 1 'm working
> 2 work
> 3 I think
> 4 'm thinking
> 5 make
> 6 'm making

4 Leave the completed sentences on the board for Clarification 1.

Clarification 1

Now or sometimes? (1)

1 Contrast Sentences 1 and 2 from the demonstration:

> 1 I can't talk now. <u>I'm working</u>.
> 2 <u>I work</u> in a café at the weekends.

Check that students can name the tenses. [1 Present Continuous. 2 Present Simple.]

9

2 Draw these timelines on the board.

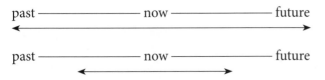

Can the students match the timelines to the tenses? [The first timeline matches Sentence 2 (the work is long-lasting or permanent). The second timeline matches Sentence 1 (the work is temporary – I'm in the middle of it now).]

* STUDENT SUPPORT If your students need help with the form and use of the Present Simple, direct them to Unit 5; for the Present Continuous they should go to Unit 4.

Thoughts, feelings and states (2)

1 Contrast Sentences 3 and 4 from the demonstration:

> 3 <u>I think</u> your job is very interesting.
> 4 <u>I'm thinking</u> about finding a new job.

In Sentence 3, **think** relates to an opinion; in Sentence 4 **think** is an action happening now. When **think** is an opinion, it is always in the Present Simple. Ask students to give other verbs which express thoughts and opinions. [E.g. **believe**, **know**.]

2 The Present Simple is also used to talk about states, e.g. *I own this book.*

* STUDENT SUPPORT To see more examples of state and action verbs, direct the students to Unit 7.

3 Contrast Sentences 5 and 6 from the demonstration:

> 5 The machines at the factory <u>make</u> a lot of noise.
> 6 I'm busy at the moment. <u>I'm making</u> sandwiches.

Ask: *Which sentence talks about a permanent fact?* [Sentence 5.] The Present Simple is used to talk about permanent facts, e.g. *Paper <u>burns</u> easily.*

4 The Present Simple is also used in **I promise**, **I agree**, **I refuse**, etc. to communicate a particular reaction, or to mean 'I do as I say': *I promise I'll write to you.*

Practice 1

Exercise A Worksheet (pairs)

WHERE'S NEIL?

- Show the worksheets to the students. Tell them they are going to read a conversation between two people

at work, Mark and Alan. Write these two 'True or False?' questions on the board:

> 1 Mark wants to speak to Neil.   *True/False*
> 2 Linda isn't working today.   *True/False*

- Divide the class into two halves. Give Student A worksheets to half the class and Student B worksheets to the other half. Give them one minute to read the conversation quickly and answer the questions 'True or False?'. Check the correct answers with the whole class. [1 False: Mark wants to speak to Linda. 2 True.]

- Give the students ten minutes to complete the exercise by putting the verbs in brackets into the correct tense, Present Simple or Present Continuous. Student As can work with other Student As at this point, and Student Bs can work together.

- Regroup the students into AB pairs. They should read the dialogue through together, checking their own answers from their partner's sheet as they do so.

- When they have finished, they can practise reading the conversation with each other. They should swap roles after the first reading.

Exercise A Extension activity (teams, pairs)
CHANGING THE FACTS

- Divide the class into teams and tell the students to turn their worksheets over.

- Tell the class you are going to test their memories. Ask the following questions about the conversation, writing them on the board as you do so:

> Who does Alan need to speak to?
> Who's Neil talking to?
> What's Neil discussing?
> How many days a week does Linda work?
> Why do Linda and Alan travel to work together by car?

- The first team to call out each correct answer wins a point. Write each answer on the board as it is called out (this is important for the next part of the activity). The team with the most points at the end wins. [Answers: 1 Neil 2 the boss 3 money 4 four 5 because they live close together or because it saves petrol]

- Direct the students to the answers on the board. Elicit alternative answers to the five questions and write them on the board. For example:

> 1 Anna
> 2 a colleague
> 3 a problem
> 4 three
> 5 because they are good friends

- Working in AB pairs again, students should read their dialogues once more; this time they should use the new facts from the board. Encourage students to be creative and make as many changes as they want, as long as they use the Present Simple and Present Continuous correctly.
- After five to ten minutes, invite confident pairs to read out their changed conversations to the whole class.

Demonstration 2

1 Write these sentences on the board or project them on an OHP. Put the students in pairs to discuss the difference in their meaning:

> 1 I'm working in a big hospital.
> 2 I work in a big hospital.

You'll check the answer in Clarification 2, so leave the sentences on the board.

Clarification 2

Temporary or permanent? (3)

1 Check the answer to the question you set in Demonstration 2. [Sentence 1 (Present Continuous) describes a situation that is seen as temporary; Sentence 2 (Present Simple) describes a situation that is seen as permanent.]

Always (4)

1 **Always** with the Present Simple means 'every time', but when it is used with the Present Continuous it means 'very often', usually with the added meaning of 'too often'. For example: *My boss is always asking me to work late.*

Note: The use of **always** isn't focused on in this lesson plan. However, if you choose to include this focus in your lesson, it is practised in Exercise C.

Practice 2

Exercise B (individuals)

- Give the students five to ten minutes to complete Exercise B, then put the students in pairs to compare their answers.
- Check the correct answers with the whole class. As you do so, check that students know why the tense is used in each answer. [E.g. Present Continuous – now; Present Continuous – temporary situation; Present Simple – habit; Present Simple – state, etc.]

Extra activity (groups)
IT'S A HARD LIFE

- Write these sentences on the board or project them on an OHP:

> 1 Where <u>do you work / are you working</u> or <u>study / studying</u>?
> 2 <u>Do you like / Are you liking</u> your job or studies?
> 3 What projects <u>do you work / are you working</u> on at the moment?
> 4 What <u>do you do / are you doing</u> on a typical Wednesday?
> 5 <u>Do you know / Are you knowing</u> where you will be this time next year?
> 6 <u>Are you worrying / Do you worry</u> about your job or studies at the moment?

- Put the students in pairs and give them a few minutes to choose the correct tense in each question. [1 do you work/study 2 Do you like 3 are you working 4 do you do 5 Do you know 6 Are you worrying]
- Put the students into small groups for five to ten minutes to discuss the questions.
- Invite some students to report back on their conversations to end the lesson.

11

Lesson 2 Worksheet

Where's Neil?

Student A

1 At work, Mark is talking to Alan in the corridor. Complete Mark's part of the conversation. Put in the Present Simple or Present Continuous of the verbs. Student B will complete Alan's part of the conversation.

Mark: Are you looking .... (you / look) for someone?

Alan: Yes, I need to speak to Neil. He isn't in his office.

Mark: (1) .... (he / talk) to the boss at the moment.

(2) .... (I / think) (3) .... (they / discuss) money.

Alan: Oh, right. And what about you? (4) Are you looking for someone too?

Mark: Yes, Linda. (5) .... (you / know) where she is?

Alan: Oh, she isn't here. She only (6) works four days a week. (7) She doesn't work on Fridays. She'll be here on Monday.

Mark: Thank you. (8) .... (you / know) a lot about Linda.

Alan: Well, most days (9) I give her a lift, or (10) she gives me one. (11) She lives quite close to me. (12) It saves petrol.

Mark: Yes, of course. Good idea. Yes, (13) .... (I / agree). Well,

(14) .... (I / waste) my time here then. I'll get back to my computer.

2 Check your answers with Student B.

✂ -

Lesson 2 Worksheet

Where's Neil?

Student B

1 At work, Alan is talking to Mark in the corridor. Complete Alan's part of the conversation. Put in the Present Simple or Present Continuous of the verbs. Student A will complete Mark's part of the conversation.

Mark: Are you looking for someone?

Alan: Yes, I need .... (I need) to speak to Neil.

Mark: (1) He's talking to the boss at the moment. (2) I think (3) they're discussing money.

Alan: Oh, right. And what about you? (4) .... (you / look) for someone too?

Mark: Yes, Linda. (5) Do you know where she is?

Alan: Oh, she isn't here. She only (6) .... (work) four days a week.

(7) .... (she / not / work) on Fridays. She'll be here on Monday.

Mark: Thank you. (8) You know a lot about Linda.

Alan: Well, most days (9) .... (I / give) her a lift, or

(10) .... (she / give) me one. (11) .... (she / live) quite close to me. (12) .... (it / save) petrol.

Mark: Yes, of course. Good idea. Yes, (13) I agree. Well, (14) I'm wasting my time here then. I'll get back to my computer.

2 Check your answers with Student A.

3 Unit 10 Past Continuous or Past Simple?

At a glance

1 This lesson reviews and contrasts:
- the **Past Continuous** to describe background events and interrupted activities in a story
- the **Past Simple** to talk about completed events and actions in the past; past states, actions or events that happen in the middle of longer events in the past; and for two actions or events that happen one after the other.

2 **Exercises A** and **B** in the book give controlled written practice in the tenses.

3 The **worksheet** '*What were you doing? and What did you do?*' provides the students with an opportunity for freer, personalized spoken practice of the Past Continuous and the Past Simple in storytelling.

Lesson length

60 minutes

Preparation

- Copy the story for the demonstration on to an OHT if you plan to use the OHP.
- Photocopy one worksheet for each student in the class.

Demonstration

1 Make sure the students have their books closed. Write the following words on the board:

> car
> night
> object
> sky
> light
> flash
> writing
> fly
> disappear

2 Tell the students that these words all come from a story told by Mike and Harriet. Ask the students to guess what happened in the story. Listen to their answers, and see if the students agree with each other. Don't focus on the accuracy of their grammar at this stage.

3 Tell the students the following summary of Mike and Harriet's story, then write it on the board or project it on an OHP:

> Mike and Harriet were driving at night. They saw a spaceship in the sky. A light was flashing on the top. It had writing on the side. As they were watching the spaceship, it flew away and disappeared.

Is it the same as the students' suggestions, or very different?

Clarification 1

Past Continuous and Past Simple (1, 2)

1 Underline the tenses in the summary on the board or OHT:

> Mike and Harriet <u>were driving</u> at night. They <u>saw</u> a spaceship in the sky. A light <u>was flashing</u> on the top. It <u>had</u> writing on the side. As they <u>were watching</u> the spaceship, it <u>flew away</u> and <u>disappeared</u>.

Remind the students that the Past Continuous and Past Simple are often used in stories.

2 The Past Simple is used for completed actions in the past. Ask the students to identify examples of completed actions in the story on the board [saw flew disappeared].

When one action happens after another we use two Past Simple verbs together. Indicate the sentence 'It flew away and disappeared.'.

3 Indicate the sentence 'It had writing on the side.'. This sentence describes a <u>state</u> in the past: the Past Simple is used to describe past states as well as past actions.

* STUDENT SUPPORT If your students need help with the form and use of the Past Simple, direct them to Unit 8.

4 We often use the Past Continuous and Past Simple together when a shorter action (or several) comes in the middle of another longer one:
While they <u>were driving</u>, they <u>saw</u> a spaceship in the sky.
As they <u>were watching</u> it, it <u>flew away</u> and <u>disappeared</u>.

5 Draw these timelines on the board and ask the students to say which of the things described in the story the different lines represent:

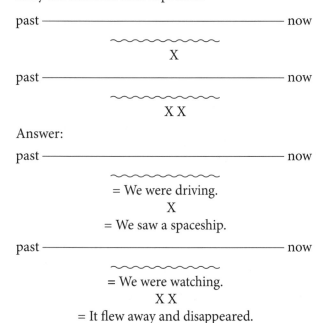

past ——————————————— now
　　　　　⌇⌇⌇⌇⌇⌇⌇⌇⌇⌇
　　　　　　　　X

past ——————————————— now
　　　　　⌇⌇⌇⌇⌇⌇⌇⌇⌇⌇
　　　　　　　X X

Answer:

past ——————————————— now
　　　　　⌇⌇⌇⌇⌇⌇⌇⌇⌇⌇
　　　= We were driving.
　　　　　　　X
　　　= We saw a spaceship.

past ——————————————— now
　　　　　⌇⌇⌇⌇⌇⌇⌇⌇⌇⌇
　　　= We were watching.
　　　　　X X
　　　= It flew away and disappeared.

6 In the example sentences, the Past Continuous comes after **while** and **as**. **When** can also be used in this position and, unlike **while** and **as**, it can be used before the Past Simple:

<u>When</u> we were driving home, we saw a spaceship.
We were driving home <u>when</u> we saw a spaceship.

* STUDENT SUPPORT If your students need help with the form and use of the Past Continuous, direct them to Unit 9.

Practice 1

Exercise A (individuals)

DAVID'S ACCIDENTS

● Ask students to close their books. Write the example questions on the board:

> when / he / carry / a suitcase / he / drop / it / on his foot
> he / break / his leg / when / he / ski

● Elicit the full sentences from the class and write the correct answers on the board:

> When he was carrying a suitcase, he dropped it on his foot.
> He broke his leg when he was skiing.

● Tell the students these sentences are both about David. Ask: *Are the sentences about holidays or accidents?* [Possibly both, but in Exercise A the sentences are all about accidents that David has had.]

● Direct the students to Exercise A and give them ten minutes to complete it. Put the students in pairs to compare answers before you check the answers with the whole class.

Exercise B (individuals, pairs)

● Ask the class: *What happens when there is a 'power cut'?* [The electricity supply in a home, a street or a group of streets stops working for some time.]

● Direct the students to Exercise B. Tell the students not to worry about the verb tenses at this stage. Give the students one minute to read the conversation and answer these two questions:
1 How long did the power cut last?
2 How many people were in the flats at the time?
[1 About ten minutes. 2 Six people: Emma, Vicky, Rachel, Matthew, Daniel and Andrew.]

● Give the students five to ten minutes to complete the exercise. Let them compare answers in pairs, then check the correct answers with the whole class.

● Put the students in pairs to practise reading the dialogues.

Exercise B Extension activity (whole class)
PAST CONTINUOUS QUESTION AND ANSWER DRILL

● Books closed. Ask the drill questions below and get the students to answer them chorally. Repeat the drill a few times until the students are producing the sentences comfortably.

T: What was Emma doing when the lights went out?
SS: She was watching television.

T: What was Rachel doing?
SS: She was coming down the stairs.

T: What were Matthew and Daniel doing?
SS: They were playing table tennis

T: What was Andrew doing?
SS: He was working on his computer

● Pay attention to the stress and rhythm of their sentences. They should pronounce **was** and **were** as /wəz/ and /wə/.

Clarification 2

Past Continuous (3)

1 Write this sentence from Mike and Harriet's story on the board:

> The stars were twinkling.

2 Ask the class: *Is this the background to <u>all</u> of Mike and Harriet's story or <u>part</u> of their story?* [All of their story.] Draw this timeline on the board:

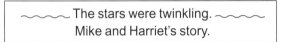

> ～～～～ The stars were twinkling. ～～～～
> Mike and Harriet's story.

Remind the students that active verbs can be used in the Past Continuous to give background information in a story.

Practice 2

Extra activity Worksheet (pairs or small groups)

WHAT WERE YOU DOING? AND *WHAT DID YOU DO?*

● Write on the board:

> Have you ever seen a spaceship?

Can anyone in the class answer 'Yes' to the question? If so, ask that student: *What were you doing? How did you feel? What did you do?* If not, ask a simpler opening question such as *Have you ever cut your finger?*, and follow it up with the same three questions.

● Show the class the worksheet and explain that there are more questions on the sheet for them to think about and answer. Check that students understand the words 'insect' and 'jellyfish'. Give one worksheet to each student in the class.

● Give the students five to ten minutes to read through the questions and make notes on their answers. Tell them that they don't need to answer every question.

● Put the students into pairs or small groups to tell each other their stories.

● After ten to fifteen minutes invite students to report back on any interesting stories that they heard.

● This worksheet could also be used as the starting point for a writing activity.

Exercise C

● Exercise C could be set for homework.

15

Lesson 3 Worksheet

What were you doing? and *What did you do?*

1 How many questions can you answer? Make notes.

a What did you dream last night?

What were you doing in your dream? ……………..……………………....……

What happened? ……………..………………………..……

b Have you ever found money (or something else valuable) in a public place?

What did you find? ……………..……………………....……

Where did you find it? ……………..……………………....……

What were you doing at the time? ……………..……………………....……

What did you do with it? ……………..……………………....……

c Have you ever had an electric shock?

What were you doing at the time? ……………..……………………....……

What happened? ……………..………………………..……

How did you feel? ……………..……………………....……

d Have you ever been camping?

Where did you go? ……………..……………………....……

What was the weather like when you arrived? ……………..……………………....……

What was the weather like for most of the holiday? ……………..……………………....……

What kind of activities did you do? ……………..……………………....……

e Have you ever been stung by an insect or jellyfish?

What were you doing at the time? ……………..……………………....……

What happened? ……………..………………………..……

How did you feel? ……………..……………………....……

What did you do? ……………..……………………....……

f Have you ever had a power cut?

What were you doing at the time? ……………..……………………....……

How long did it last? ……………..……………………....……

What did you do? ……………..……………………....……

2 Tell one or more of your stories to other students. Work in pairs or small groups.

4 Unit 14 Present Perfect or Past Simple? (1)

At a glance

1 This lesson reviews and contrasts:
- the **Present Perfect** to talk about and give news of recent events and changes
- the **Past Simple** with time markers like **yesterday**, **last year**, and **ten minutes ago** to talk about when things happened in the past, and to give more information about recent events and changes.

2 The **worksheet '*I have done* or *I did?*'** is an adaptation of **Exercise A** in the book and gives the students controlled written practice of the two tenses in the form of a pair-work activity.

3 **Exercise B** in the book gives the students further controlled written practice.

4 The **extra activity 'The news'** gives the students the opportunity for freer, written practice of the Present Perfect and the Past Simple.

Lesson length

45–60 minutes

Preparation

- Photocopy one worksheet for each pair of students. Cut the worksheets in half.

Demonstration 1

1 Write these two sentences on the board:

> 1 It's started to rain.
> 2 Someone has called the police!

Tell the students to look at the sentences and to think about situations in which each would mean good news or bad news. [Suggested answers: 1 Good news if you're in a country that needs rain; bad news if you're going to have a picnic. 2 Good news if you need help; bad news if you're a criminal.]

Leave the two sentences on the board for Clarification 1.

Clarification 1

I have done or *I did?* (1)

1 Ask the students: *What tense is used in the sentences on the board?* [The Present Perfect.] *What time do the sentences refer to – to recent time, or time in the past which is finished?* [Recent time.] The Present Perfect tells us about the past and the present; the event happened in the past, but it has a significance now.

2 Check that the students understand this concept: ask them to look again at the two sentences on the board and say what the significance is now. [Suggested

answers: 1 It's raining now, and the ground is wet. 2 The police are coming.]

* STUDENT SUPPORT If your students need help with the form and use of the Present Perfect, direct them to Unit 11.

3 We use the Past Simple (not the Present Perfect) to talk about finished times in the past such as **yesterday**, **last week**, **in 1994**, **100 years ago**. Compare:

1 *It's started to rain.* and *It started to rain at seven o'clock.*
2 *Someone has called the police!* and *Someone called the police five minutes ago.*

The timing of the event is the same, but the speakers' views of the event are different: the use of the Past Simple with a past time phrase (**at seven o'clock**, **five minutes ago**) indicates that the speaker sees the event as finished, whereas the use of the Present Perfect shows that the speaker sees the event as connected to now.

Practice 1

Exercise A (two teams)

WARM-UP

- Draw the following noughts and crosses grid on the board:

start	buy	do
run	lose	go up
make	earn	break

- Arrange students in two teams, Os and Xs. Teams take turns to choose a verb and toss a coin. If the coin lands face up, the team has to make a sentence using the Past Simple. If the coin lands face down, the team makes a Present Perfect sentence. If the sentence is correct, put an X or O in the appropriate square. Teams compete to make a line of Os or Xs to fill the square.

- Play another round using the same verbs, or different ones from Exercise A.

Exercise A Worksheet (pairs)
I HAVE DONE OR I DID?

- Show the worksheets to the students and explain that they will be working on different versions of the same worksheet. Divide the class into two halves. Give Student A worksheets to half the class and Student B worksheets to the other half.
- Give the students ten minutes to complete the exercise by putting the verbs in brackets into the correct tense, Present Perfect or Past Simple. Student As can work with other Student As at this point, and Student Bs can work together.
- They should then get their partner to test them and tell them if they are right.
- At the end of the exercise, go through the sheet with the whole class, to make sure that they all have a correct set of answers.

Demonstration 2

1 Write these speech statements on the board:

> 1 She's had a little boy.
> 2 Firefighters have entered the building.

Put the students in pairs to discuss where and when you might hear these pieces of news. [Suggested answers: 1 From friends or family when a baby is born. 2 On the TV or radio when there is a fire or there has been an explosion.]

Leave the two sentences on the board for Clarification 2.

Clarification 2

I've done it. I did it yesterday. (2)

1 Point out that we often give a piece of news in the Present Perfect. We use the Past Simple to give or ask details, such as when and where something happened.

2 Ask the class to think of some information that could be added to the news on the board. Make sure the students use the Past Simple. [Suggested answers: 1 He was born at 4.30 this morning. He weighed

about 3 kilos. 2 The fire started in the kitchen. It spread quickly to other rooms.]

Structures with for, since and last (3)

1 We use **for** and **since** with the negative Present Perfect to talk about the last time an action happened:
We haven't had a party for ages. We haven't had a party since Christmas.

2 The same ideas can be expressed with a positive form of the Past Simple:
It's ages since we last had a party. Christmas was the last time we had a party.

* STUDENT SUPPORT For more information on the Present Perfect with **for** and **since**, direct the students to Unit 12.2.

Note: These structures aren't focused on in this lesson plan. However, if you choose to include this focus in your lesson, Exercise C provides controlled practice.

Practice 2

Exercise B (individuals)

- Ask the students to close their books. Write the prompts for the first sentence in Exercise B on the board:

> the Prime Minister / visit Luton University / speak to students there / earlier today.

Tell the students that this is some information about a story on the radio news. They need to use the words to make two sentences – one to give the news, and the other to give a further detail about the story. Elicit the correct answer from the students and write it on the board:

> The Prime Minister has visited Luton University. He spoke to students there earlier today.

- Give the students ten minutes to complete Exercise B. Go round the class as they work to give help where needed.
- Let students compare their answers in pairs before you check the correct answers with the whole class.

Extra activity Worksheet (groups)
THE NEWS

- Direct the students to the news headlines on the worksheet. Make sure they understand 'survive', 'jungle', and 'Celebrity'.

- Put the students into small groups. Ask them to choose three of the four headlines. For each one, they must write a short news report. Tell them to write one Present Perfect sentence to give the news for each story. Then ask them to write two or three Past Simple sentences with details about each story. Give the students ten to fifteen minutes to do this, and go round the class to look at their work and give support or guidance where groups need it.
- When all the groups are ready, they can read out and compare their news reports.

Lesson 4 Worksheet

Student A

I have done or *I did?*

Write the correct form of the verb in brackets ( ).

	The news

The news

Four survive in the jungle for a week

Footballer in prison

Scientists discover new animal

Celebrity agrees to teach English class

1 Our visitors .... (arrive). They're sitting in the garden.

2 There's still a problem with the television. Someone ....
(repair) it, but then it broke down again.

3 .... (I / lose) my bank card. I can't find it anywhere.

4 The match .... (start). United are playing well.

5 My sister .... (run) away from home. But she came back two
days later.

6 Daniel .... (earn) some money last week. But I'm afraid he's
already spent it all.

Answers for Student B
7 We planted an apple tree in the garden. Unfortunately, it died.
8 Prices have gone up. Everything is more expensive this year.
9 Someone has turned on the hi-fi. What's that song called?
10 I phoned the office at eleven to speak to the manager, but he isn't
   there today.
11 I've made a cake. Would you like a piece?
12 The runner Amos Temila broke the world record for the 1500 metres in
   Frankfurt. Then, two days later in Helsinki, Lee Williams ran it in an even
   faster time.

Lesson 4 Worksheet

Student B

I have done or *I did?*

Write the correct form of the verb in brackets ( ).

The news

Four survive in the jungle for a week

Footballer in prison

Scientists discover new animal

Celebrity agrees to teach English class

7 .... (we / plant) an apple tree in the garden. Unfortunately it
died.

8 Prices .... (go) up. Everything is more expensive this year.

9 Someone .... (turn) on the hi-fi. What's that song called?

10 .... (I / phone) the office at eleven to speak to the manager,
but he isn't there today.

11 .... (I / make) a cake. Would you like a piece?

12 The runner Amos Temila .... (break) the world record
for the 1500 metres in Frankfurt. Then, two days later in Helsinki, Lee
Williams ran it in an even faster time.

Answers for Student A
1 Our visitors have arrived. They're sitting in the garden.
2 There's still a problem with the television. Someone repaired it, but then it
   broke down again.
3 I've lost my bank card. I can't find it anywhere.
4 The match has started. United are playing well.
5 My sister ran away from home. But she came back two days later.
6 Daniel earned some money last week. But I'm afraid he's already spent it all.

5 Unit 19 Review of the Past Simple, Continuous and Perfect

At a glance

1 This lesson reviews and contrasts the use of the **Past Simple**, **Past Continuous** and **Past Perfect** in narratives.

2 The **Reading** exercise on the **worksheet 'Good-luck and bad-luck stories'** tests the students' understanding of the use of the three tenses.

3 **Exercise C** in the book gives controlled written practice of tenses in a 'good-luck' story.

4 **Storytelling** on the worksheet **'Good-luck and bad-luck stories'** provides the students with an opportunity for freer and creative spoken and/or written practice.

Lesson length

45–60 minutes

Preparation

- Make one copy of the worksheet for each student in the class.

Demonstration

1 Write this question on the board:

> Do you think you generally have good luck or bad luck?

Make sure everyone understands the question then put the students into pairs or threes to discuss it for a minute or two. When the groups are ready, ask the 'lucky' people and then the 'unlucky' people to put their hands up. Tell the class they are going to be reading and telling good- and bad-luck stories in this lesson.

Worksheet (individuals, groups)
GOOD-LUCK AND BAD-LUCK STORIES – READING

1 Hand out the worksheet and make sure the students all have their books closed. Give them a minute to read the text and choose the best title for the story. Tell them not to worry about the grammar at this point.

2 Let the students discuss their answer with a partner, then check the correct answers with the whole class. [c An Expensive Crime.]

3 Ask: *Was the young man in the story lucky or unlucky?* [Unlucky.]

4 Check that the students understand these words: 'checkout', 'cashier', 'till', 'snatched'. Now give the students five minutes to read the story again and

choose the correct tenses. Let the students compare answers in pairs. They'll see the correct answers in the clarification stage.

Clarification 1

Introduction (1)

1 Direct the students to the Introduction on page 44 in the book to check their answers. Remind the students that usually when we tell a story we need to combine different past tenses – the Past Simple, the Past Continuous and the Past Perfect.

Past Simple + Past Simple (2)

1 Ask: *What happened when the cashier opened the till?* Write the sentence on the board and underline the Past Simple:

> The man <u>snatched</u> the money and <u>ran</u> out of the store.

2 Draw this timeline on the board:

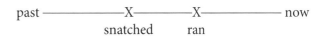

past ————————X————————X——————— now
            snatched   ran

Ask: *Did these things happen at the same time?* [No. One action happened and then the next one happened.]

* STUDENT SUPPORT If your students need more help with the form and use of the Past Simple, direct them to Unit 8.

Past Continuous + time/event; Past Continuous + Past Simple (2, 3)

1 Ask: *Was the shop busy at the time?* Write this sentence on the board and underline the Past Continuous:

> No. At the time of the incident, not many people <u>were shopping</u> in the store.

2 Draw this timeline on the board:

the incident
past ————————————X———————————— now
not many people were shopping

The Past Continuous gives information <u>around</u> a past time or past event.

3 The Past Continuous can also be used in combination with the Past Simple to give information around a past action. For example:

> I <u>was waiting</u> at the checkout when I <u>noticed</u> a strange-looking man.

Ask: *Which was the longer action?* [waiting] *What tense is used for the shorter action?* [The Past Simple.]

* STUDENT SUPPORT If your students need more help with the form and use of the Past Continuous, direct them to Unit 9.

Extra activity (whole class)
PROMPT DRILL

1 Use this prompt drill to break up the clarification and to give your students very controlled practice of the Past Continuous and the Past Simple.

T: Was the store busy? No, …
SS: No, not many people were shopping in the store.

T: Was the checkout busy? No, …
SS: No, no one else was waiting at the checkout.

T: What was the security guard doing? She …
SS: She was standing at the other end of the store.

T: He / walk into a supermarket / take a basket
He …
SS: He walked into a supermarket and took a basket.

T: She / open the till / he snatch the money She …
SS: She opened the till and he snatched the money.

T: He / snatch the money / run out of the store
He …
SS: He snatched the money and ran out of the store.

2 Go through the drill a few times until the students can produce the sentences comfortably.

Clarification 2

Past Simple + Past Perfect (2, 4)

1 Ask: *What did the staff discover when they checked the records?* Write this sentence on the board and underline the Past Simple and Past Perfect:

> They <u>found</u> that the thief <u>had taken</u> only £4.37.

2 Ask: *Which event happened first – 'find' or 'take'?* [take] Draw this timeline on the board:

past ——————————X————————X——————————— now
took £4.37 They found

We use the Past Perfect for things <u>before</u> a past situation. It can also be used in the same way in the second of two sentences:

A man walked into supermarket. He had chosen a quiet time. = He chose a quiet time before he walked into the supermarket.

* STUDENT SUPPORT If your students need more help with the basic form and use of the Past Perfect, direct them to Unit 18.

3 We can also use the Past Perfect followed by the Past Simple to emphasize the sequence of two actions. In this case, we use **when** or **after**, and the events in the sentence are mentioned in the order that they happened. For example:

<u>When</u> he <u>had filled</u> his basket, he went to the checkout.
<u>After</u> he <u>had filled</u> his basket, he went to the checkout.

4 It is also possible to use the Past Simple after **after** with the same meaning, but not after **when**. For example:

<u>After</u> he <u>filled</u> his basket, he went to the checkout.
~~*When he filled his basket, he went to the checkout.*~~

5 We can use the Past Perfect and Past Simple with **before** and **until**. There is no difference in meaning. For example:

He arrived at the store <u>before</u> it <u>had opened</u> / <u>opened</u>.
He stayed at the store <u>until</u> he <u>had taken</u> the money from the till / <u>until</u> he <u>took</u> the money from the till.

Practice

Exercise C (individuals)

● Give the class a minute to read the story in Exercise C and to answer this question:
Is this a good-luck story or a bad-luck story?

- Tell the students not to worry about the grammar at this point. Check the correct answer with the whole class. [A good-luck story.]
- Now give the students five minutes to read the story again and complete the grammar exercise. Let the students compare answers in pairs before you go through the correct answers with the whole class.

Extra activity Worksheet (individuals, groups)
GOOD-LUCK AND BAD-LUCK STORIES – STORYTELLING

- Direct the students to the storytelling section on the worksheet and tell them to study the two different story patterns.
- Tell the students that they are going to prepare and tell a simple good-luck or bad-luck story. Get them to suggest what kind of events they could write about. You could write these ideas on the board to get the students started:

| a journey |
| an exam |
| a meal |
| an accident |
| a conversation |

- Give the class five to ten minutes to think about their stories and make notes. Let them use bilingual dictionaries to research any vocabulary that they need. Go round the class as the students work, so that you can be a source of help and support.
- When the students are ready, put them into small groups to tell each other their stories. Alternatively, students could write their stories out and then pass them round for each other to read.
- At the end of the lesson, ask students to say which were the luckiest and unluckiest stories they had heard (or read).

Exercises A and B

- Exercises A and B could be set for homework.

Lesson 5 Worksheet

Good-luck and bad-luck stories

Reading

1 Read the text and choose the best title for the story.

a A Clever Thief [ ]

b Security Man Stops Thief [ ]

c An Expensive Crime [ ]

2 Now read the text again and <u>underline</u> the correct tense, Past Simple, Past Continuous or Past Perfect.

A young man <u>*walked*</u> / *was walking* into a supermarket in Southampton and [1] *put / was putting* a few items of food in a basket. He [2] *had chosen / was choosing* a time when not many people were shopping in the store. He found a checkout where no one else [3] *was waiting / had waited*. When the cashier had checked the goods, the man [4] *gave / had given* her a £10 note. When she opened the till, the man quickly snatched all the money from it and [5] *was running / ran* out of the store before she realized what [6] *happened / was happening*. At the time the security guard [7] *was standing / stood* at the other end of the store. When staff checked the records in the till, they [8] *found / had found* that the thief [9] *had taken / took* only £4.37. As he [10] *had left / was leaving* the £10 note behind, the operation had cost him £5.63.

3 Compare your answers with a partner, then look at the correct text on page 44.

Storytelling

1 Choose one of the story patterns below. Make notes. Write or tell your story to other students. Use the Past Simple, Past Continuous and Past Perfect in your stories.

Story Pattern 1: A bad-luck story

Where were you?
What were you trying to do?
What went wrong?
How did you feel afterwards?

Story Pattern 2: A good-luck story

Where were you?
What problem did you have?
How did people help you?
How did you feel afterwards?

---

6 Unit 27 When I get there, before you leave, etc.

At a glance

1 This lesson focuses on the linking words **when, before, as soon as, while**, etc., used with the **Present Simple** to talk about future time.

2 **Exercise B** in the book provides controlled written practice of linking word + **will** or the Present Simple.

3 'Linking words' on the **worksheet** gives further controlled practice of the different linking words presented in the lesson.

4 'Go by bike or take a taxi?' on the **worksheet** gives the students the opportunity for freer spoken practice in the form of two role plays.

Lesson length

50 minutes

Preparation

- Copy the questions for the demonstration and Practice 2 on to an OHT if you plan to use the OHP.
- Photocopy one worksheet for each student in the class.

Demonstration

1 Ask the class: *How do people usually travel when they are on business?* [By train, plane or car.] Tell the class they are going to read a conversation between Mark and his wife Sarah about Mark's business trip. Write these four questions on the board or project them on an OHP:

> 1 Where is Mark's meeting tomorrow morning?
> 2 How is he going to get there?
> 3 What does Sarah think about this plan?
> 4 Why does Mark think his plan is a good idea?

2 Direct the students to the conversation at the top of page 66 in the book. Give them one minute to read the conversation quickly and answer the questions. Check the correct answers with the whole class. [1 Glasgow 2 by car 3 She thinks it's crazy. 4 He needs the car in Glasgow.]

Clarification 1

Present Simple with a future meaning (1)

1 Ask the students to close their books. Write on the board:

> Sarah: You'll be exhausted before …
> Mark: I'll need the car while …
> Mark: I can sleep when …

Can the students complete the sentences from memory? Write the answers on the board and underline the second clause in each sentence:

> Sarah: You'll be exhausted before <u>you arrive</u>.
> Mark: I'll need the car while <u>I'm there</u>.
> Mark: I can sleep when <u>I get home</u>.

Ask: *Are these sentences about now or the future?* [The future.] *What tense is the verb after the link words in each sentence?* [The Present Simple.]

2 We can also start a sentence with some (but not all) of the linking words in this lesson:

> Mark: <u>When I get home</u>, I can sleep.

Practice 1

Extra activity (pairs)
READING A CONVERSATION

- To break up the clarification, put the students in pairs for a minute or two to practise reading the conversation between Mark and Sarah on page 66.

Clarification 2

Linking words (2)

1 Write these four linking words on the board:

before	as	as soon as	after

Draw these four timelines on the board:

1 now ——— arrive ——— do it ———— future

2 now ——— arrive - do it ———— future

3 now — do it — arrive ———————— future

4 now _____ arrive _____ future
         do it

2 Read out these four sentences and ask the students to match them to the timelines on the board:

A *I'll do it before I arrive.*
B *I'll do it as I arrive.*
C *I'll do it as soon as I arrive.*
D *I'll do it after I arrive.*
[A3 B4 C2 D1]

3 Write these other linking words on the board:

> by the time
> until
> when
> while

By the time is often used with the Future Perfect, and is represented by Timeline 3. For example: *I'll have done it by the time I arrive.*

Until can also be represented by Timeline 3. For example: *I'll do it until I arrive.*

When is similar to **as soon as**, but means more generally 'some time after'. It is represented by Timeline 2. For example: *I'll do it when I arrive.*

To use **while**, the sentence would need to be changed to *I'll do it while I'm there.*

4 Remind the students that we also use the Present Simple with a future meaning after the conditional marker **if**.

* STUDENT SUPPORT For more information on **If** + Present Simple + future, direct the students to Unit 144.1–3.

Linking words with the Present Perfect and Present Continuous (3, 4)

1 After linking words of time, we can often use the Present Perfect in the same way as the Present Simple. For example:

I'm starting a job in sales after I've finished college. As soon as you've heard any news, will you let me know?

2 Sometimes the meaning is the same as when the Present Simple is used, but sometimes there is a difference in meaning. For example:
When I see the report, I'll make some notes. (I'll do both at the same time.)
When I've seen the report, I'll make some notes. (I'll see it and then make notes.)

3 We can also use the Present Continuous after a linking word, especially after **when** and **while**. For example: *I'm going to listen to the radio while I'm cooking.*

4 Exercise C can be set at this point if you want to give your students controlled written practice of linking words with the Present Perfect and Present Continuous.

Practice 2

Exercise B (individuals, pairs)

● Give the students about five minutes to complete Exercise B. Let the students compare answers in pairs before you go through the correct answers with the whole class.

● Write these three questions on the board or project them on an OHP:

> 1 What will Mark do to stay awake?
> 2 What's he going to do this evening?
> 3 What will he do in the morning?

● Check the correct answers with the whole class and encourage them to use a linking word + Present Continuous / Present Simple / Present Perfect in the answers. [1 He'll listen to music while he's driving. 2 He'll lie down for a couple of hours before he leaves. 3 He'll phone Sarah when he's arrived.]

● Put the students in pairs to practise reading the conversation.

Exercise B Extension activity Worksheet (pairs)
LINKING WORDS

● Ask the students to close their books. Put the students in pairs and direct them to the two exercises on linking words on the worksheet. All the sentences come from the text and Exercise B in the book. Give the students ten minutes to complete the exercises.

● When they have finished, the pairs can check their answers by looking at pages 66 and 67.

Extra activity Worksheet (pairs)
GO BY BIKE OR TAKE A TAXI? – ROLE PLAYS

● Divide the class into AA and BB pairs and tell them to look at Role Play 1.

● All the As should prepare Anita's part of the conversation, and all the Bs should prepare James's part of the conversation. To do this, they should look at the ideas in the table and prepare what they are going to say. They should try to include some of the different linking words from the lesson in their sentences (e.g. *It might start to rain while you're cycling. I'll phone you as soon as I get to the cinema.*)

- Reorganize the students into AB pairs and give them a few minutes to conduct their role plays.
- When all the pairs have finished, invite one or two pairs to perform their conversation in front of the whole class.
- Repeat the procedure with Role Play 2.

Exercise A

- Exercise A could be set for homework.

Lesson 6 Worksheet

Linking words

1 Match the two parts of Sarah's sentences.

1 You'll be exhausted before ___c___
2 If you take a train, _____
3 If you need a car, _____
4 I'll be worried _____
5 But don't ring before _____
6 You'll be exhausted tomorrow _____

a I'm awake in the morning.
b if you don't get some sleep this evening.
c ~~you arrive.~~
d it'll be much more comfortable.
e until I hear from you.
f you can hire one when you get to Glasgow.

2 Now complete Mark's sentences with linking words from the box.

As soon as   before   If   ~~while~~   when   when

1 I'll need the car ____while____ I'm there.
2 _____ I hire a car, it will be too complicated.
3 I'll get there much quicker _____ there's no traffic on the road.
4 I can sleep _____ I get home.
5 _____ I arrive, I'll ring you, I promise.
6 I'll lie down for a couple of hours _____ I go.

3 Check your answers by looking on pages 66 and 67.

Go by bike or take a taxi?

Look at the information below, and imagine you are the people in the situations. You will have two conversations about the situations (one in each role play). Remember to use linking words, the Present Simple, and **will** in your conversations.

Role Play 1:
Go by bike or take a taxi?

Situation: Anita wants to ride to the cinema in the city centre on her bicycle. James thinks this is a bad idea.

Student A: Anita	Student B: James
You think ...	**You think ...**
• you will be quicker on a bike, especially in bad traffic	• riding a bicycle in the city centre is dangerous
• it's cheaper than a taxi	• a taxi is quicker and more comfortable
• you will phone James from the cinema immediately	• it might start to rain
	• you will be worried

Student A should begin the conversation by saying, 'I'm going to go to the cinema by bike.'

Role Play 2:
Ride a motorbike or walk?

Situation: Adam is going on holiday to a small island with some friends next month. He wants to hire a motorbike on holiday. Kate thinks this is a bad idea.

Student A: Kate	Student B: Adam
You think ...	**You think ...**
• riding a motorbike is dangerous	• riding a motorbike will be fun
• walking is safer and cheaper	• you'll need a motorbike on the island
• the roads on the island might be very bad	• you will have some motorbike lessons this month
• you will buy some new walking shoes for Adam before the holiday	• if necessary, you'll phone Kate

Student B should begin the conversation by saying, 'I'm going to hire a motorbike on holiday.'

7 Unit 37 Subject/object questions

At a glance

1 This lesson focuses on the use and form of **subject and object questions**. It includes questions with:
- **who** and **what**
- **which, whose, how many** and **how much.**

2 **Exercise C** in the book gives controlled written practice of subject and object questions with **who** and **what.**

3 **Exercise B** provides practice of subject and object questions with **which, whose, how many** and **how much.**

4 The **worksheet 'Tell me more'** provides the opportunity for freer, personalized written and spoken practice of the lesson content.

Lesson length

45–60 minutes

Preparation

- Prepare an OHT for Demonstration 1 if you plan to use the OHP.
- Photocopy one worksheet for each student in the class.

Demonstration 1

1 Ask the class: *How do you feel when the telephone rings at three o'clock in the morning?* and elicit a few answers.

2 Write this conversation on the board or project it on an OHP:

> Someone phoned me at three o'clock this morning.
> Oh? Who _____ ?
> My friend Tom. He told me something important.
> Really? What _____ ?

Put the students in pairs to read the conversation and complete the two questions. When the students have finished, write the two questions on the board:

> Who phoned you?
> What did he tell you?

3 Leave the two questions on the board for the clarification. To close this stage, ask the class to suggest some reasons why Tom may have phoned in the middle of the night.

Clarification 1

Who and what (1)

1 Underline **who** and **what** in the two questions:

> 1 <u>Who</u> phoned you?
> 2 <u>What</u> did he tell you?

2 Ask: *Is 'who' the subject or object of Question 1?* [The subject.] *Is 'what' the subject or object of Question 2?* [The object.] To reinforce this, show how **who** and **what** relate to **someone** and **something** in these sentences:

> Subject
> <u>Someone</u> phoned me.
> Subject
> <u>Who</u> phoned you?
> Subject
> <u>X</u> phoned me.
>   Object
> He told me <u>something</u>.
> Object
> <u>What</u> did he tell you?
>   Object
> He told me <u>X</u>.

3 Highlight the form to the students. The word order of a subject question is the same as in a statement. In an object question, an auxiliary (e.g. **did, will**) comes before the subject.

4 Ask students: *Can 'who' also refer to the object of the sentence?* [Yes.] and *Can 'what' also refer to the subject of the sentence?* [Yes.] Write these examples and elicit the missing subject questions:

> Subject
> <u>Something</u>'s happened.
>
> Subject
> _____?
>
> Subject
> <u>X</u> has happened.
>
>   Object
> I'm going to tell <u>someone</u>.
>
> Object
> _____?
>
>   Object
> I'm going to tell <u>X</u>.

[Answers: <u>What</u>'s happened? <u>Who</u> are you going to tell? Note: In formal English, **whom** is sometimes used: <u>Whom</u> are you going to tell?]

5 **Who** and **what** can also be the object of a preposition. For example: *Who were you talking <u>to</u>? What does this colour go <u>with</u>?*

Practice 1

Exercise B (individuals)

- Give the students five to ten minutes to complete Exercise B. Let the students compare answers in pairs before you check the answers with the whole class.

Exercise B Extension activity (whole class)
CUE/RESPONSE DRILL

- Extend Exercise B with this drill to give the students very controlled practice in producing subject and object questions with **who** and **what**.
- Books closed. Read the lines from Exercise B. After each line, students should respond with the appropriate subject or object question. For example:

  T: Something has happened.
  SS: What has happened?

  T: I've invited someone for tea.
  SS Who have you invited?

  T: Somebody is having a party.
  SS Who is having a party?
  etc.

- Go through the drill a couple of times, until the students are producing the questions comfortably.

Clarification 2

Which, whose, how many and how much (2)

1 Write **which**, **whose**, **how many** and **how much** on the board. Tell the students that these words can also be either the subject or the object of a question. They are usually followed by a noun.

2 Say some prompt sentences to elicit the relevant subject and object questions. For example:

   T: One of the programs will work best.
   SS: Which program will work best? [Subject question.]

   T: Melanie is walking someone's dog.
   SS: Whose dog is Melanie walking? [Object question.]

   T: Some oil got in the river.
   SS: How much oil got in the river? [Subject question.]

   For more prompt sentences and examples, see Section 2 on page 90.

Practice 2

Exercise C (individuals)

- Give the students five to ten minutes to complete Exercise C. Let the students compare answers in pairs before you check the answers with the whole class.

Exercise C Extension activity (groups)
TEST YOUR PARTNER

- Extend Exercise C with this activity. Divide the class into AB pairs. Student A closes his/her book. Student B reads Harriet's lines. Student A tries to remember Mrs Evans's lines. When Student A produces the correct question, Student B can supply the answer. For example:

  Student A: So, ten people have sent cards?
  Student B: How many people have sent cards?
  Student A: Ten.

- After a few minutes, A and B should reverse roles.

Extra activity Worksheet (pairs)
TELL ME MORE

- Write on the board:

I cooked something yesterday.

- Ask the class to suggest subject or object questions to find out more information.
- Show the class the worksheet and explain that they are going to be using subject and object questions to find out information from each other.

- Hand out the worksheets and give the students a few minutes to read the sentences and tick the ones which are true for them.
- Divide the class into pairs. Tell the students to look at each other's worksheets. They now have five minutes to write questions to find out more information about the sentences that their partner has ticked. Go round the class as the students work to give support and correct errors where necessary.
- When the students have prepared their questions, they should use them to interview their partner.
- To close the activity, invite students to report back on what they found out about each other.

Lesson 7 Worksheet

Tell me more

1 Read the sentences. Tick ✓ the sentences which are true for you.

  1 I cooked something yesterday. [ ]
  2 Someone sent me an email yesterday. [ ]
  3 Someone phoned me yesterday. [ ]
  4 I phoned someone yesterday. [ ]
  5 I bought something last weekend. [ ]
  6 Something good happened yesterday. [ ]
  7 My friend gave me something for my last birthday. [ ]
  8 Someone took a photo of me last week. [ ]
  9 I spent too much money last weekend. [ ]
 10 I've learnt a lot in the last few years. [ ]
 11 I'm going to visit someone next summer. [ ]
 12 Someone in my family is going to have a baby soon. [ ]
 13 I've got lots of brothers and sisters. [ ]
 14 Lots of people came to my party last year. [ ]
 15 One of my feet is bigger than the other. [ ]
 16 I need to change something in my life. [ ]
 17 Someone's book is in my bag. [ ]
 18 I'm going to someone's house this evening. [ ]

2 Read your partner's sentences. Prepare questions to find out more information. For example:

  9 I spent too much money last weekend. ✓
     .How..much..did..you..spend?.....

3 Ask your partner the questions.

8 Unit 43 So/Neither do I and I think so

Lesson length

45–60 minutes

Preparation

- Make one copy of the worksheet for each student in the class.

Demonstration 1

1 Write these two statements on the board:

> People are all the same.
> People are all very different.

Ask the students to consider which sentence they agree with more. Let them discuss their answers in pairs for a minute or so, then get some feedback from the class on what they think.

2 Tell the class that the first part of the lesson focuses on people talking about what they have in common – i.e. their similarities.

3 Write this conversation on the board:

> I don't like this cold weather.
> 1 _____ .
>
> I like warm weather.
> 2 _____ .

Two people are taking part in the conversation. The second speaker feels the same as the first speaker. Ask the class if they know how the second speaker can express his or her feelings.

4 When the students are ready, write the correct answers on the board:

> 1 Neither do I.   2 So do I.

Leave the sentences on the board for Clarification 1.

Note: Students may offer the sentences *I don't like this cold weather either.* and *I like warm weather too.* These sentences are also appropriate, but not focused on in this lesson.

Clarification 1

So and neither (1)

1 **So** and **neither** are used to show agreement and similarity. We use **so** after a positive statement and **neither** after a negative one. **So do I** means 'I do too' and **neither do I** means 'I don't either'.

2 Highlight the form on the board:

> So/Neither + auxiliary + subject
> Neither   do   I.
> So   do   I.

3 Other auxiliaries can be used in this structure, as well as other subjects. Give some other examples: *neither can they, so will I, neither did we, so could she*, etc. Get the students to practise saying sentences after you. Make sure they stress **so/neither** and the subject: <u>neither</u> can <u>they</u>, <u>so</u> will <u>I</u>, <u>neither</u> did <u>we</u>, etc.

4 We can use **nor** instead of **neither**. For example, *nor do I, nor can they.*

5 The structure can either be used on its own, as part of a conversation (as in Demonstration 1), or as a clause at the end of a sentence. For example: *I went to the party and so did John. David can't drive, and neither can Melanie.*

Practice 1

Exercise A (individuals, pairs)

- Give the students about five minutes to complete Exercise A. Let the students compare answers in pairs before you check the correct answers with the whole class.
- Keep the students in pairs to practise reading the conversation.

Exercise B (individuals)

- Direct the students to Exercise B. Make sure they understand what the table represents. Give them about five minutes to complete the exercise. Let the students compare answers in pairs before you check the correct answers with the whole class.

Extra activity Worksheet (groups)

SIMILARITIES AND DIFFERENCES – EXERCISES 1 AND 2

- Give one worksheet to each student in the class. Direct the students to Exercise 1. Give them a few minutes to read the statements and tick the ones which are true for them.
- Divide the class into groups. Students should talk to each other to find what they have in common. At this stage, they can use the conversational structures *so can I, neither am I*, etc.

  Note: Point out to the class that when they find <u>differences</u> between themselves, they can say: *Oh, I do! Oh, I can't*, etc.

- When the students have finished discovering their similarities, give them five to ten minutes to make sentences with clauses at the end using **so** and **neither/nor** (like the sentences in Exercise B). For example: *I've got lots of books and so has Sasha. I'm not keen on sport, and neither is Becky.*
- Go round the class as the students work to support and correct as necessary.
- When everyone has finished, invite students to read out some of their sentences.

Demonstration 2

1 Write these two statements on the board, with a line after each for a response:

> I think it's going to snow tomorrow.
> _____ (☺)
>
> I think it's going to snow tomorrow.
> _____ (☹)

Ask the class to suggest how the two people might respond differently to the snow statement.

2 When the class is ready, write these two responses on the board:

> I hope so! ☺
>
> I hope not! ☹

Leave the sentences on the board for Clarification 2.

Clarification 2

I think so, etc. (2)

1 Here **I hope so!** means 'I hope it snows tomorrow' and **I hope not!** means 'I hope it doesn't snow tomorrow'.

2 We can use **so** in this way after **be afraid, believe, expect, guess, hope, suppose** and **think**. These verbs express hopes, fears, beliefs and other attitudes. Check that students know the meanings of these verbs.

3 There are two negative structures. With **expect** and **think**, we normally use the negative and **so**: *Is it raining? ~ I <u>don't think so</u>. Are you going to the concert? ~ I <u>don't expect so</u>.*

  With **be afraid, guess** and **hope**, we use the positive and **not**: *Is it raining? ~ I <u>hope not</u>. Have we won a prize? ~ I'<u>m afraid not</u>.*

4 We can't use **so** after **know** or **be sure**: *We're late. ~ I know. Are you sure this is the right way? ~ Yes, I'm sure.*

5 With **so** structures, the verb is stressed: *I <u>expect</u> so, I <u>hope</u> so, I don't <u>think</u> so*, etc. In structures with **not**, the stress is on **not**: *I'm afraid <u>not</u>, I suppose <u>not</u>.*

Practice 2

Exercise C (individuals)

- Direct the students to Exercise C in the book. Give them about five minutes to complete the exercise. Let the students compare answers in pairs before you check the correct answers with the whole class.

Extra activity Worksheet (groups/mingling)

SIMILARITIES AND DIFFERENCES – EXERCISES 3 AND 4

- Direct students to Exercise 3 on the worksheet. Give them a few minutes to complete the table, allowing them to check their own answers by looking on page 104 in the book. Go through the answers with the whole class by reading out the positive statements and getting the students to respond each time with a negative one. Make sure the students are saying the sentences with the correct stress (see Clarification 2).

- Give the students about five to ten minutes to read the questions in Exercise 4 and to add an appropriate response to each one according to how they feel.
- Invite the students to get up and move around the class, asking each other the questions. They should make a note of who has given the same responses as them. (If it is not feasible to get the students moving around, put them into groups.)
- At the end of the activity, invite students to report back on whether people generally had the same or different responses.

Lesson 8 Worksheet

Similarities and differences

1 Tick the statements that are true for you.

I'm not keen on sport. ☐ ....
I've got lots of books. ☐ ....
I can't dive. ☐ ....
I love cats. ☐ ....
I don't have to get up early tomorrow. ☐ ....
I cook quite often. ☐ ....
I've been to New York. ☐ ....
I don't have much free time. ☐ ....

2 Talk to other students and find people who ticked the same statements. Make sentences like the ones in Exercise B in the book.

3 Complete the negative responses. (Look on page 104 if you're not sure.)

Positive	Negative
I hope so.	I _hope not_ .
I think so.	I ....
I believe so.	I ....
I guess so.	I ....
I expect so.	I ....
I suppose so.	I ....
I'm afraid so.	I' ....

4 Look at the questions below. Use the positive and negative expressions in the table above to answer each question.

1 Is it warm outside? ....

2 Are you doing anything special this evening? ....

3 Is your best friend working today? ....

4 Are you going on holiday this year? ....

5 Are you good at cooking? ....

6 Are you good at mathematics? ....

7 Will you ever be famous? ....

8 Will you be living in the same place this time next year? ....

9 Will you be doing the same job or studies this time next year? ....

10 Will you have a lot of grandchildren? ....

Ask other students the questions. Can you find someone with three responses that are the same as yours? Five? More than five?

9 Unit 46 Possibility and certainty: may, might, could, must, etc.

At a glance

1 This lesson clarifies the use of modal verbs for talking about **possibility and certainty** including:
- **may**, **might** and **could** for present and future possibility
- **could not** and **could never** for present and future impossibility
- **must** and **can't** for present certainty.

2 **Exercise B** is adapted as a drill to practise **may** and **might**.

3 **Exercise D** gives controlled written practice in talking about possibility and certainty.

4 The **worksheet 'You must be joking!'** gives further practice of the language within a functional context.

Lesson length

50 minutes

Preparation

- Copy the sentences for the demonstration on to an OHT if you plan to use the OHP.
- Make a copy of the worksheet for each student in the class.

Demonstration

1 Write these sentences on the board or project them on the OHP:

> 1 It might rain.
> 2 That bottle may fall.
> 3 He might be in the garden.
> 4 You could win £1 million!
> 5 That story could be true.
> 6 I can't do that!
> 7 I could never do that!
> 8 Your phone must be in the car.
> 9 He can't be tired yet.

Tell the class these sentences are all about possibility and certainty. Put the students in pairs and give them a few minutes to discuss whether each sentence is about now or the future.

2 Check the correct answers with the whole class and write the time against each sentence:

> 1 future 2 future 3 now 4 future 5 now
> 6 now 7 future 8 now 9 now

Leave the sentences on the board for the clarification stages.

Clarification 1

may, might and could (1)

1 Highlight the modal verbs **may** and **might** in Sentences 1 to 3 from the demonstration:

> 1 It <u>might</u> rain. future
> 2 That bottle <u>may</u> fall. future
> 3 He <u>might</u> be in the garden. now

2 We use **may** or **might** (+ infinitive without **to**) to say that something is possible or that it is quite likely. We can use them for the present or the future. Show the students how the sentences on the board can change:

> 1 It <u>might/may</u> rain.
> 2 That bottle <u>may/might</u> fall.
> 3 He <u>might/may</u> be in the garden.

3 Highlight **could** in Sentences 4 and 5 from the demonstration:

> 4 You <u>could</u> win £1 million! future
> 5 That story <u>could</u> be true. now

Like **may** and **might**, **could** is also used to say that something is possible now or in the future. Ask the students: *When we use 'could', do we think the possibility is big or small?* [Small, compared to **may** and **might**.]

Note: When we think an activity is possibly in progress now, we can use a continuous form (**be** + **-ing**) after **may**, **might** and **could**. For example: *He might be sitting in the garden.*

Practice 1

Exercise B (whole class)
TRANSFORMATION DRILL

- Use Exercise B in the book as a transformation drill with the whole class to give the students very controlled oral practice in **may** and **might**. First, get the students to transform all the sentences using **may**. Make sure the students have their books closed and are looking at and listening to you.

  T: I'm not sure if it's going to rain.
  SS: It may rain.

  T: I don't know if we'll see an elephant.
  SS: We may see one.

  T: I can't say whether Daniel will win.
  SS: Daniel may win.

  etc.

  Then repeat the drill with might:

  T: I'm not sure if it's going to rain.
  SS: It might rain.

  T: I don't know if we'll see an elephant.
  SS: We might see one.

  T: I can't say whether Daniel will win.
  SS: Daniel might win.

  etc.

- Go through all of the sentences in Exercise B with **may** and **might** until the students can produce them comfortably.

Clarification 2

may, might and could in the negative (2)

1 The negative forms of **may** and **might** are **may not** and **might not / mightn't**. This means that something negative is possible. For example: *He might not be* in the garden. *He may not get* the job.

2 Highlight **can't** and **could never** in Sentences 6 and 7 from the demonstration:

> 6 I can't do that! now
> 7 I could never do that! future

3 When something is impossible now, we use **can't**. To talk about something that is impossible now or in the future, we use **couldn't** or **could never**.

Exercise B

- Exercise B can be set at this point if you want to give your students controlled written practice of **mightn't** and **couldn't**.

Clarification 3

must and can't (3)

1 Highlight **must** and **can't** in Sentences 8 and 9 from the demonstration:

> 8 Your phone must be in the car. now
> 9 He can't be tired yet. now

Ask the class: *Are these sentences about possibility or certainty?* [Certainty.] *100 per cent certainty or 99 per cent certainty?* [99 per cent certainty – if we are 100 per cent certain we say *Your phone is in the car.* and *He isn't tired yet.*]

We use **must** when we realize that something is certainly true. We use **can't** when we realize that something is certainly impossible.

2 Like **may**, **might,** and **could**, **must** and **can't** can also be followed by a continuous form. For example: *Andrew isn't here. He must be working in the library.*

Practice 2

Exercise D (individuals)

- Tell the class they are going to read a conversation between a TV reporter and a woman called Mrs Miles. Write these two 'True or False?' questions on the board:

> 1 Mrs Miles is going to do a parachute jump. True/False
> 2 The reporter would like to do a parachute jump. True/False

- Give the students one minute to read the conversation quickly and answer the questions 'True or False?'. Check the correct answers with the whole class [1 True 2 False].
- Give the students a few minutes to complete Exercise D. Let them compare their answers in pairs, then check the correct answers with the whole class.

Extra activity Worksheet (pairs)
YOU MUST BE JOKING!

- Tell the class that **may, might, could, must,** etc. are used commonly in everyday expressions in spoken English. Hand out the worksheet, and look at the example statement and response with the whole class.
- Put the students in pairs, and give them about five minutes to complete the exercise. Check the correct answers with the whole class [1a 2b 3c 4a 5c 6c 7a].

- Get the students to practise saying the expressions with lots of feeling!
- Put the students in pairs again, and get them to choose two or three of the conversations and develop them further using their own ideas.
- Invite confident pairs to perform their conversations in front of the whole class.

Lesson 9 Worksheet

You must be joking!

Choose the best response to each sentence.

My parents are getting divorced.	a ~ That must be difficult for you. ✓ b ~ You can't be serious. [ ] c ~ You might win. [ ]
1 Is it true that you're a millionaire?	a ~ You must be joking! [ ] b ~ That can't be true, surely. [ ] c ~ You might not like it. [ ]
2 I think we should sell the house.	a ~ That must be terrible. [ ] b ~ You can't be serious! [ ] c ~ You might enjoy it! [ ]
3 I'm going to do a parachute jump.	a ~ That must be terrible. [ ] b ~ That can't be true, surely. [ ] c ~ I could never do that! [ ]
4 I've lost my job and my wife is ill.	a ~ Life can't be very easy for you. [ ] b ~ You must be joking! [ ] c ~ You might be right. [ ]
5 I've never watched a football match and I don't want to watch one now!	a ~ You must be so angry! [ ] b ~ Your life can't be much fun. [ ] c ~ You might enjoy it! [ ]
6 I think you should tell him the truth.	a ~ You must be so happy! [ ] b ~ Your life can't be much fun. [ ] c ~ I could never do that! [ ]
7 We're going to have another baby.	a ~ You must be so happy! [ ] b ~ That can't be true, surely. [ ] c ~ I could never do that! [ ]

1 This lesson focuses on the function of **asking people to do things**, with:

- **Can you …?, Could we …?, Do you mind …?, Would you mind …?, I wonder if you could …**
- **the imperative**
- asking for things with **Can I/we …?** and **Could I/we …?**

The lesson also presents ways of responding to requests.

2 **Exercises A** and **B** in the book provide controlled written practice of the structures.

3 The **worksheet 'Out and about'** gives further practice of the lesson input in the context of mini-dialogues in different social settings.

Lesson length

45–60 minutes

Preparation

- Copy one worksheet for each student in the class.

Demonstration 1

1 Play this game with the students. Tell them you are going to give them some instructions. They should listen to all the instructions, but only respond to the ones which are polite.

Can you open your books at page 121, please?
Look at me!
Could you pick up your pens, please?
Stand up!
Would you mind standing up, please?
Sit down!
I wonder if you could sit down now, please.
Would you like to look at the board, please?

See if you can catch the students out by getting them to respond to the imperative requests!

Clarification 1

Polite requests (1)

1 Write the five polite requests from the demonstration on the board and underline the structures that make the sentences polite:

> <u>Can you</u> open your books at page 121, please?
> <u>Could you</u> pick up your pens, please?
> <u>Would you mind</u> standing up, please?
> <u>I wonder if you could</u> sit down now, please.
> <u>Would you like to</u> look at the board, please?

2 Point out that it is important to use these request forms in English. Requests without these structures can sound very abrupt and impolite.

Ask: *Which is more polite, 'can' or 'could'?* [could]. Point out that it is possible to say **Do you mind …?** as well as **Would you mind …?** in a polite request. Ask: *Which is more polite, 'do' or 'would'?* [would]. Ask: *Which is the most polite structure on the board?* [I wonder if you could …].

3 Check that students know how to respond to the polite requests you have presented so far.

Can/Could you …?
I wonder if you could …
Would you like to …?
Example 'yes' response: ~ *Yes, of course.*
Example 'no' response: ~ *I'm afraid I can't at the moment.*

Do/Would you mind …ing …?
Example 'yes' response: ~ *No, that's fine.*
Example 'no' response: ~ *I'd rather not, I'm afraid.*

4 Get the students to repeat the polite requests and responses in order to practise the pronunciation.

The imperative (2)

1 Write the three imperative sentences from the demonstration on the board:

> Look at me!
> Stand up!
> Sit down!

We can use the imperative form to tell someone what to do, but it is not formal or polite. Even people in authority often avoid using the imperative to give orders. Instead they can use **I want / I'd like you to …**, **You must …**, or a polite request form, e.g.:

I want you all to be at the meeting. You must stop at the red light. Could you open your mouth, please?

Ask: *When can we use the imperative?* [We can use the imperative when we are with friends in an informal situation. We use the imperative in instructions and directions (*Turn right here.*), in offers and invitations (*Have a biscuit.*), and to express good wishes (*Enjoy your holiday.*).]

2 Check that students can form the negative imperative: *Don't look at me! Don't stand up! Don't sit down!*

Practice 1

Extra activity (whole class)
SUBSTITUTION DRILL

● Give the students very controlled practice with this substitution drill.

T: Open the door! **Can …**
SS: Can you open the door?

T: **close …**
SS: Can you close the door?

T: **Could / please …**
SS: Could you close the door, please?

T: **wonder …**
SS: I wonder if you could close the door, please.

T: **window …**
SS: I wonder if you could close the window, please.

T: **Would / mind …**
SS: Would you mind closing the window, please?

T: **clean …**
SS: Would you mind cleaning the window, please?

● Go through the drill a few times until the students are producing the requests naturally and politely.

Demonstration 2

1 Repeat the game from Demonstration 1. This time, ask individual students for things:

Raoul, give me your pen.
Antonia, could I have a pen, please?
Sara, give me your book.
Pavel, can I have your book, please?

Clarification 2

Asking for things (3)

1 Write these two polite requests on the board and underline the structures that make them polite:

> Could I have a pen, please?
> Can I have your book, please?

Could/Can we is also possible.

We can also say *Could you give me a pen, please?*, but we do not use the imperative.

2 When we ask for something in a shop or café we can simply name what we want, but we must say **please**: *A large white loaf, please. Two coffees, please.*

We can also use **I'd like …** or **I'll have …**: *I'd like a sandwich, please. I'll have a coffee, please.*

3 Check that students know how to respond to the polite requests you have presented in this part of the lesson.

Can/Could I …?
Example 'yes' response: ~ *Yes, of course.*
Example 'no' response: ~ *I'm afraid …* (+ reason, e.g. *… I need it at the moment.* or *… I haven't got one.*).

I'll have … / I'd like …
Example 'yes' response: ~ *Certainly. Here you are.*
Example 'no' response: ~ *I'm afraid ….* (+ reason).

Practice 2

Exercise A (whole class)

● Direct the students to Exercise A in the book. Go through the exercise with the whole class, and repeat the requests in order to practise the pronunciation.

Exercise A Extension activity (open pairs)

● Extend Exercise A with this open pair-work activity. Invite pairs of students to make and respond to offers across the class. To begin with they can use the pictures in Exercise A as prompts, but they should vary the request structures that they use. They can then make up their own requests.
● This exercise could also be done in closed pairs.

Exercise B (individuals, pairs)

● Direct the students to Exercise B in the book. Make sure students realize that they only need to put one word in each line to complete the exercise. Give them five to ten minutes to complete the exercise. Let the students compare answers in pairs before you check the correct answers with the whole class.
● Put the students in pairs to practise reading the requests and responding to them.

Extra activity Worksheet (pairs)
OUT AND ABOUT

- Give a worksheet to each student in the class. Divide the class into pairs and tell them to match the dialogues to the contexts given in the box. Which pair can do this most quickly? Check the answers with the whole class [b in the office c in the street d in a café e on the phone f in a shop].
- Give the pairs five to ten minutes to rewrite the requests so that they are more polite. Go round the room as the students are working so that you can check their work. (Students can use any of the request forms from the lesson at this stage.)
- Get the students to practise reading their dialogues. Encourage them to add the reason that B gives at the end of each dialogue for not fulfilling the request.
- Invite different pairs to read out one or two of their dialogues at the end.

Exercise C

- Exercise C could be set for homework.

Lesson 10 Worksheet

Out and about

1 Read the dialogues below. Match the contexts to the dialogues.

in a café   in the office   ~~at home~~   in a shop   on the phone   in the street

a *at home*

    A Answer the phone!
    B I can't at the moment.

b

    A Photocopy this report, Linda.
    B Certainly.
    A And work until 6 o'clock this evening.
    B I can't do that, I'm afraid.

c

    A Tell me the way to Victoria Station.
    B Of course. Just turn right here and keep walking.
    A Come with me.
    B I can't I'm afraid.

d

    A Give me a cheese sandwich.
    B Here you are. And would you like a drink with that?
    A I want a coffee.
    B I'm afraid that's not possible at the moment.

e

    A I want to speak to James.
    B He's not here at the moment.
    A Take a message.
    B I can't I'm afraid.

f

    A I want this book.
    B OK, that's £6 please.
    A Give me a bag.
    B I'm afraid that's not possible.

2 Now rewrite A's lines so that they are more polite.

3 Practise reading the dialogues with a partner. How does each dialogue end?

At a glance

1 This lesson focuses on the structure **have something done** for talking about:
- professional services
- unpleasant experiences.

It also focuses on the related structure **get something done** for professional services.

2 **Exercises A**, **B**, **C** and **D** in the book give controlled written practice of **have something done** and **get something done**.

3 Exercise 1 on the **worksheet 'Services and experiences'** provides the students with further written practice of the language in mini-conversations.

4 Exercise 2 on the **worksheet** provides the students with an opportunity to activate all the language from the lesson in freer, personalized practice.

Lesson length

50 minutes

Preparation

- Photocopy one worksheet for each student in the class.

Demonstration

1 Inform the class you're going to tell them about a trip into town. They should listen and write down two good things that happened, and one bad thing.

Last week I went into town to do some things. I had my hair cut and I got some invitations printed for the party next summer. It was a pleasant afternoon. But when I got home I had a shock. I realized I'd had my bag stolen.

Let the students discuss their answers in pairs before you check with the whole class. [Two good things: hair cut and invitations; one bad thing: bag stolen.] You may notice that the students are or are not using **have something done** at this point, but don't focus on the grammar yet.

Clarification 1

Have/get something done (1, 2, 3)

1 At this point, just write the two good things from the story on the board:

> I had my hair cut.
> I got some invitations printed.

Ask: *Did I cut my hair?* [No.] *Who cut it?* [A hairdresser.] *Did I pay the hairdresser?* [Yes.] *Did I*

print the invitations? [No.] *Who printed them?* [A printer.] *Did I pay the printer?* [Yes.]

Tell the students that this is a particular kind of passive structure, used commonly in spoken English. It is used to talk about something done for us as a service. These services are things that we choose and arrange with professionals.

2 Ask: *Which is more formal, 'have something done' or 'get something done'?* [have something done]

3 Highlight the form:

Subject + have/get + something + done			
I	had	my hair	cut.
I	got	some invitations	printed.

Show the students how this pattern works with different tenses, with modal verbs, and in the negative form:

Subject + have/get + something + done			
My friend 's having	his hair	cut next week.	
I	might get	some more invitations	printed.
I	didn't have	my suit	cleaned.

Show the students the question form:

(Question word +) auxiliary + subject + have/get + something + done				
Where should	I	have	my hair	cut?
Did		you get	your suit	cleaned?

Practice 1

Exercise A (pairs)

- Put the students in pairs to complete Exercise A, then check the answers with the whole class.

Exercise A Extension activity (whole class)
PICTURE PROMPT DRILL

- Extend Exercise A with this picture prompt drill to give the students very controlled oral practice. The students will need to look at the book but also listen to you for the time prompt.

  T: Trevor / yesterday **He ...**
  SS: He had his hair cut yesterday.

  T: Mike / at the moment **He ...**
  SS: He's having his car serviced.

  T: Melissa / yesterday **She ...**
  SS: She had her photo taken.

  T: David / today **He ...**
  SS: He's having his windows cleaned.

  T: Rachel / going to ... / tomorrow **She ...**
  SS: She's going to have her eyes tested.

- Go through the drill a few times until the students are producing the sentences comfortably.

Clarification 2

Have something done meaning 'experience something bad' (4)

1 Ask the students: *What was the <u>bad</u> thing that happened in the story?* Write the sentence on the board:

> I had my bag stolen.

2 Ask: *Did I want this to happen?* [No.] *Did I pay for this to happen?* [No.] The **have something done** structure can also be used with the meaning 'experience something'. It usually refers to something unpleasant and unwanted.

This is a much less common use of the **have something done** structure.

Practice 2

Exercise D (pairs)

- Put the students in pairs and give them five minutes to complete Exercise D. Check the answers with the whole class.

Extra activity Worksheet (pairs)
SERVICES AND EXPERIENCES – EXERCISE 1

- Write the jobs from the worksheet on the board:

  > car mechanic
  > optician
  > hairdresser
  > dentist
  > decorator
  > window cleaner

- Ask the students:
  Which professional services do you use?
  Which of these jobs would you like to do?
  Which of these jobs wouldn't you like to do?

- Give a worksheet to each student in the class and direct them to Exercise 1A. Divide the class into pairs and tell them to match the dialogues to jobs in the box (they will complete the sentences in Exercise 1B). Which pair can do this most quickly? Check the answers with the whole class [2 h 3 g 4 a 5 b 6 f].

- Give the pairs five to ten minutes to complete Exercise 1B. Check the answers with the whole class [2 get them cleaned 3 have it decorated 4 'm having it serviced 5 get them tested 6 have it taken out].

- Get the students to practise reading the conversations with their partner.

Extra activity Worksheet (pairs)
SERVICES AND EXPERIENCES – EXERCISE 2

- Direct the students to Exercise 2A on the worksheet. Give them five minutes to complete the questions. Let them compare their answers in pairs before you check the correct answers with the whole class. [1 had a tooth taken out or filled 2 have your photo taken 3 had your portrait drawn or painted 4 had your luggage searched 5 had something stolen]

- Working in the same pairs, the students should interview each other using the **have something done** questions and also the follow-up questions ('How did you feel?' 'Who took it?' 'Where?', etc.).

- At the end of the activity, get feedback by asking questions like:
  Whose partner has had a tooth taken out or filled?
  Whose partner has had their photo taken recently?

- Get the students to report to the rest of the class what they have found out about each other.

Exercises B and C

- Exercises B and C could be set for homework.

Lesson 11 Worksheet

Services and experiences

1 Professional services

A Read the six conversations quickly and match them to these jobs:

| a car mechanic   b optician   c ~~hairdresser~~   f dentist   g decorator   h window cleaner |

1
  A Your hair looks different. It's nice. ..hairdresser....
  B Thanks. .I've just had it cut............ .

2
  A The windows are really dirty! ....
  B I know. We should ....

3
  A I don't like the colour of the kitchen. ....
  B Perhaps we should ....

4
  A Where's your car? ....
  B It's at the garage. I ....

5
  A I can't read this. My eyes are really bad. ....
  B You should ....

6
  A My tooth really hurts, but I don't want to go to the clinic. ....
  B Why not?
  A I don't want to .... !

B Read the conversations again and complete them with phrases from the box.

| get them cleaned | ~~I've just had it cut~~ | have it decorated |
| 'm having it serviced | have it taken out | get them tested |

2 Speaking

A Complete the questions using the words in brackets ( ).

1 Have you ever .... (have / a tooth / take out or fill)?
How did you feel?

2 When did you last .... (have / your photo / take)?
Who took it? Where?

3 Have you ever .... (have / your portrait / draw or paint) by a
street artist? Were you happy with the result?

4 Have you ever .... (have / your luggage / search) by customs?
When? Where? How did you feel?

5 Have you ever .... (have / something / stolen)?
What was it? Where did it happen?

B Interview your partner using the questions.

12 Unit 62 Verb + to-infinitive or verb + -ing form?

At a glance

1 This lesson presents a number of verbs which are:
- followed by **the to-infinitive** (e.g. **beg, demand, pretend**)
- followed by **the -ing form** (e.g. **avoid, imagine, risk**).

2 **Exercise A** in the book gives controlled written practice.

3 **'Making a complaint in a shop'** on the worksheet **'Shops and services'** is an adaptation of **Exercise B** in the book. It gives the students controlled written practice of the verb forms in a pair-work format.

4 **'What kind of consumer are you?'** on the **worksheet** provides the students with an opportunity for further controlled written practice and then freer, personalized spoken practice of the lesson input.

Lesson length

50 minutes

Preparation

- Copy the mini-questionnaire for the demonstration on to an OHT if you plan to use the OHP.
- Photocopy one worksheet for each pair of students. Cut the worksheets in half.

Demonstration

1 Write this mini-questionnaire on the board or project it on an OHP:

> 1 I avoid going to the shops
>
> _____
>
> (a) when I haven't got much money. (b) when I'm hungry. (c) as much as possible!
>
> 2 I hope to have a _____
>   holiday next year.
> (a) skiing (b) beach (c) cheap (d) long
> (e) romantic

Put the students into groups of three to discuss their answers for a couple of minutes. Briefly get some feedback from the groups on their responses.

Clarification

Verb + to-infinitive or verb + -ing form? (1, 2)

1 Highlight the verb patterns in the sentences on the board:

verb + -ing form
I <u>avoid</u> <u>going</u> to the shops when I'm hungry.
verb + to-infinitive
I <u>hope</u> <u>to have</u> a long holiday next year.

2 Point out that some verbs are followed by a to-infinitive, and some by an -ing form. Write the following table and verbs on the board:

+ to-infinitive (e.g. *to go*)	+ -ing form (e.g. *going*)
hope	avoid
imagine appear arrange practise offer threaten delay prepare deny risk	

Books closed. Tell the students to copy the table on to a piece of paper and to put the verbs into the correct place. They can do this with a partner.

3 After a few minutes, let the students check their answers by looking at page 148 (Section 2). Write the correct answers on the board too:

+ to-infinitive (e.g. *to go*)	+ -ing form (e.g. *going*)
appear arrange prepare offer threaten	imagine practise risk delay deny

4 Point out that there are many verbs like this; some are presented in this lesson but others the students will have to learn as they encounter them as new pieces of vocabulary in the future.

5 A few verbs take either a to-infinitive or an -ing form.

* STUDENT SUPPORT For more information on verbs which can take either a to-infinitive or an -ing form, direct the students to Units 63 and 64.

Can't wait and fancy (3)

1 If you **can't wait** to do something, you are eager to do it. It is followed by the to-infinitive. For example:

I can't wait to see the photos you took. = I really want to see them.

2 If you **fancy** doing something, you want to do it. It is followed by the -ing form. For example:

Do you fancy going out for a meal? = Would you like to go out for a meal?

Note: **fancy** is informal.

Happen, turn out and prove (4)

1 We use **prove** or **turn out** when experience shows what something is like. **Prove** and **turn out** are both followed by the to-infinitive. For example:

My prediction proved to be correct.
The job turned out to be more difficult than I thought.

2 Note the meaning of **happen** with the to-infinitive:

I happened to see Sarah in town. = I saw Sarah by chance in town.

Two forms together (5)

1 We can sometimes use more than one to-infinitive or -ing form together. Write this on the board:

> The government decided <u>refuse / give in</u> to the terrorists.
> I want <u>avoid / hurt</u> anyone's feelings.
> The man denied <u>threaten / kill</u> a policeman.

Can the class form the sentences correctly?

2 When they are ready, write the answers on the board:

> The government decided <u>to refuse to give in</u> to the terrorists.
> I want <u>to avoid hurting</u> anyone's feelings.
> The man denied <u>threatening to kill</u> a policeman.

Note: The use of two forms together isn't focused on in this lesson plan. However, if you choose to include this focus in your lesson, Exercise C provides controlled practice.

Practice

Exercise A (individuals)

● Tell the class they are going to read a conversation between some friends about going on holiday. Write these questions on the board:

> 1 Which two countries do they talk about?
> 2 Who is worried about money?

● Give the students one minute to read the conversation in Exercise A quickly and answer the questions. Check the correct answers with the whole class [1 Greece and Scotland. 2 Jessica.]

● Give the students a few minutes to complete **Exercise A**. Let them compare their answers in pairs, then check the correct answers with the whole class.

Worksheet (pairs)
MAKING A COMPLAINT IN A SHOP

● Find out if anyone in the class has ever made a complaint in a shop or restaurant. What was the problem? How did they deal with it? What was the result? Tell the class they're going to read a text about making a complaint in a shop.

● Books closed. Divide the class into two groups, Group A and Group B. Give a copy of the Student A worksheet to all the students in Group A, and the Student B worksheet to all the students in Group B. Direct them to the first exercise, 'Making a complaint in a shop'. Give them five minutes to read the text and to complete it with the correct form of the verbs in the instructions. Students can work in AA and BB pairs at this stage.

● Reorganize the class into AB pairs. They can check their answers collaboratively by looking at each other's worksheets.

Extra activity Worksheet (pairs)
WHAT KIND OF CONSUMER ARE YOU?

● Direct students to the second exercise on the worksheet, 'What kind of consumer are you?'. Give them a few minutes to complete their five questions individually by putting the verbs into the correct form. They can refer to the information on page 148 (Section 2) in the book for help.

● Put the students into AB pairs again. Give them five minutes to interview each other using the questions they have just completed. Invite pairs to report back on whether their answers were similar or very different, and to give some examples.

Lesson 12 Worksheet

Shops and services

Student A

Making a complaint in a shop

1 Complete this article from a magazine. Put in the to-infinitive or -ing form of these verbs: *accept, be, insist, plug, take, wait.*

If you buy something from a shop, a new stereo for example, you usually can't wait .to. plug........ it in and put some music on. And of course, you expect **to find** the equipment in working order. But that doesn't always happen, unfortunately. If the thing doesn't work, you should take it straight back to the shop. If you delay [1]................. it back, you will risk **losing** your rights as a customer. And you should prepare [2].................. on those rights. You may be one of those people who always avoid **arguing** with people, but in this case you should be ready for an argument. The assistant may prove [3].................. a true friend of the customer – it's not impossible – but first he or she will probably offer **to repair** the stereo for you. That's all right if you don't mind [4].................. a few weeks, but it isn't usually a good idea.

What you should do is politely demand **to have** your money back immediately. You may want to accept another stereo in place of the old one, but you don't have to. You should refuse [5].................. a credit note. Just keep on **saying** that you want your money back.

2 Check your answers with Student B.

What kind of consumer are you?

1 Complete the sentences below with the to-infinitive or -ing form of the verbs.

1 I enjoy .... (*shop*) for things like stereos, mobile phones and computer equipment. *Agree / Disagree*

2 I tend .... (*go shop*) alone for clothes. *Agree / Disagree*

3 I don't mind .... (*pay*) more money for good quality in shops and restaurants. *Agree / Disagree*

4 I once spent a lot of money on something that turned out .... (*be*) a complete waste of money. *Agree / Disagree*

5 I resent .... (*pay*) money for treatment by doctors and dentists. *Agree / Disagree*

2 Do you agree or disagree with each statement?

3 Read your statements to Student B. Does he / she agree or disagree with the statements?

Lesson 12 Worksheet

Shops and services

Student B

Making a complaint in a shop

1 Complete this article from a magazine. Put in the to-infinitive or -ing form of these verbs: *argue, find, have, lose, repair, say.*

If you buy something from a shop, a new stereo for example, you usually can't wait **to plug** it in and put some music on. And of course, you expect .to. find........ the equipment in working order. But that doesn't always happen, unfortunately. If the thing doesn't work, you should take it straight back to the shop. If you delay **taking** it back, you will risk [1].................. your rights as a customer. And you should prepare **to insist** on those rights. You may be one of those people who always avoid [2].................. with people, but in this case you should be ready for an argument. The assistant may prove **to be** a true friend of the customer – it's not impossible – but first he or she will probably offer [3].................. the stereo for you. That's all right if you don't mind **waiting** a few weeks, but it isn't usually a good idea.

What you should do is politely demand [4].................. your money back immediately. You may want to accept another stereo in place of the old one, but you don't have to. You should refuse **to accept** a credit note. Just keep on [5].................. that you want your money back.

2 Check your answers with Student A.

What kind of consumer are you?

1 Complete the sentences below with the to-infinitive or -ing form of the verbs.

1 I detest .... (*shop*) for clothes and shoes. *Agree / Disagree*

2 I can't help .... (*spend*) too much money when I go to the shops. *Agree / Disagree*

3 I've never refused .... (*pay*) for a meal in a restaurant because it was so bad. *Agree / Disagree*

4 I can't afford .... (*buy*) a lot of things that I really want. *Agree / Disagree*

5 I would never consider .... (*buy*) anything on the internet. *Agree / Disagree*

2 Do you agree or disagree with each statement?

3 Read your statements to Student A. Does he / she agree or disagree with the statements?

13 Unit 64 Remember, regret, try, etc.

At a glance

1 This lesson focuses on verbs such as **remember** and **regret** which can be followed either by the **to-infinitive** or the **-ing form**, but with a difference in meaning.

2 The **worksheet 'Same verb, different meaning'** is a pair-work activity which tests the students' knowledge of this language area.

3 **Exercises A** and **C** in the book provide controlled written practice.

4 The **extra activity 'Speaking'** provides an opportunity for freer, personalized practice of the language.

Lesson length

50 minutes

Preparation

- Photocopy one worksheet for each pair of students. Cut the worksheets in half.
- Copy the sentences for the extra activity on to an OHT if you plan to use the OHP.

Demonstration 1

1 As a lead-in, ask the class: *Do you have a good memory? Do you find it easy to remember telephone numbers? What about everyday things that you need to do? Events from childhood? What you did last week?*

2 Write these sentences on the board:

> A I must remember / <u>post</u> this letter today. It's important.
> B I can remember / <u>post</u> the letter. I posted it on Friday morning.
> C The clothes are still dirty because I forgot / <u>switch</u> on the machine.
> D I'll never forget / <u>fly</u> over the Grand Canyon. It was wonderful.

Tell the students to read the sentences. Ask: *What form should the second verb in each sentence be: the to-infinitive or the -ing form?* When the students have thought about it, write the correct answers on the board:

> A I must remember <u>to post</u> this letter today. It's important.
> B I can remember <u>posting</u> the letter. I posted it on Friday morning.
> C The clothes are still dirty because I forgot <u>to switch</u> on the machine.
> D I'll never forget <u>flying</u> over the Grand Canyon. It was wonderful.

Leave the sentences on the board for Clarification 1.

Clarification 1

Remember and forget (1)

1 Some verbs, like **want** and **hope**, are followed by a to-infinitive; others, like **enjoy**, are followed by an -ing form.

* STUDENT SUPPORT For more information on verb + to-infinitive or verb + -ing form, direct the students to Unit 62.

Other verbs, like **remember** and **forget**, can take either a to-infinitive or an -ing form, but the choice depends on the meaning.

2 Compare:

> A I must remember <u>to post</u> this letter today.
> B I can remember <u>posting</u> the letter.

Ask: *In Sentence A, which happens first, 'remember' or 'post'?* ['remember': If I remember, I'll post the letter.] *And in Sentence B?* ['post': I posted the letter; now I remember that.]

3 Compare:

> C … I forgot <u>to switch</u> on the machine.
> D I'll never forget <u>flying</u> over the Grand Canyon.

51

Ask: *In which sentence is 'forget' about a memory of the past?* [Sentence D.] *In Sentence C, did I switch on the machine?* [No.]

remember/forget + to-infinitive
= think / not think about a necessary action
remember/forget + -ing
= think / not think about a memory of the past

Practice 1

Exercise A (individuals, pairs)

- Set Exercise A to give the students practice in choosing between the to-infinitive and the -ing form after **remember** and **forget**. Tell the class they are going to read a short conversation between Laura and Trevor. Tell them to read the first few lines of the conversation to answer this question: *Who always forgets things – Trevor or Laura?*
- Check the correct answer with the whole class [Trevor].
- Give the students about five minutes to complete Exercise A. Let them compare their answers in pairs before you check the correct answers with the whole class.
- Put the students in pairs to practise reading the conversation with a partner.

Worksheet (pairs)

SAME VERB, DIFFERENT MEANING

- Tell the class they are now going to study more verbs which can be followed by the to-infinitive or the -ing form, with a difference in meaning.
  Books closed. Divide the class into two groups, Group A and Group B. Give a copy of the Student A worksheet to all the students in Group A, and the Student B worksheet to all the students in Group B. Give them five to ten minutes to choose the to-infinitive or the -ing form to complete each sentence. Within the groups, students can work in pairs (i.e. AA, BB).
- When everyone is ready, reorganize the class into AB pairs to compare their answers. When Student A has an -ing form answer, then Student B should have a to-infinitive answer, and vice versa. If they have the same -ed or -ing answer, then one of them is wrong. In this case, they need to look at their sentences together to see which answer needs to be changed. For final confirmation of their answers, all the students should look at page 152 of the book.

Clarification 2

1 Contrast the sentences from the worksheet. Use the concept-check questions below to check that all the students understand how the choice of the to-infinitive or an -ing form after each of these verbs affects the meaning.

Regret (2)

A *We regret to inform you …*
B *I regret spending all that money.*

Ask: *In which sentence is the speaker sorry about a past action?* [B] *What is the speaker sorry about in A?* [An action now – in this case, giving bad news.]

regret + to-infinitive = feel sorry about something now
regret + -ing = feel sorry about something you did or didn't do in the past

Try (3)

A *I'm trying to run this computer program.*
B *I tried clicking on the box …*

Ask: *Which sentence is about doing something in order to see what happens?* [B] *In A, is the computer program easy or difficult to run?* [Difficult.]

try + to-infinitive = attempt something difficult
try + -ing = experiment.

Stop (4)

A *Stop talking please.*
B *He stopped to talk to us.*

Ask: *Which sentence answers the question 'Why'?* [B. Why did he stop? In order to talk to us.]

stop + to-infinitive = finish one action in order to do another
stop + -ing = end an action.

Mean (5)

A *Applying for a visa means filling in this form.*
B *He meant to break that glass.*
Ask: *Which sentence is about a neutral consequence and which is about a personal intention?* [A = neutral consequence. B = intention.]

mean + to-infinitive = intend
mean + -ing = have something that follows as a consequence.

Go on (6)

A *She introduced herself, then she went on to explain about the course.*
B *Everyone went on talking.*

Ask: *In Sentence A does the activity change or stay the same?* [It changes.] *And in Sentence B?* [It stays the same.]

go on + to-infinitive = change to a new activity
go on + -ing = continue with the same activity.

Need (7)

A *My shoes <u>need cleaning</u>.*
B *I <u>need to clean</u> my shoes.*

Ask: *In Sentence B, who needs to clean my shoes?* [Me.] *In Sentence A, who needs to clean my shoes?* [It could be anyone: me, someone else, or even a machine.]

need + -ing = passive meaning. Here it means 'My shoes need to be cleaned (by someone or something).'
need + to-infinitive = active meaning.

Practice 2

Exercise C (individuals)

● Give the students five to ten minutes to complete Exercise C. Let them compare answers in pairs before you check the correct answers with the whole class.

Extra activity (groups)
SPEAKING

● Write these sentences on the board or project them on the OHP:

> 1 Have you ever completely forgotten / <u>do</u> something really important?
> 2 Are you going on / <u>do</u> something else after this lesson?
> 3 Are you planning to go on / <u>learn</u> English when this course finishes?
> 4 Have you ever tried / <u>record</u> yourself speaking English?
> 5 Do your shoes need / <u>clean</u> at the moment?
> 6 What do you need / <u>do</u> this evening?
> 7 Do you remember / <u>meet</u> your best friend for the first time?

Go through the correct answers with the whole class [1 to do 2 to do 3 learning 4 recording 5 cleaning 6 to do 7 meeting].

● Put the students into small groups to discuss their answers to the questions.
● To close the lesson, get some students to report back on what they found out about each other.

Exercise B

● Exercise B could be set for homework.

Lesson 13 Worksheet

Same verb, different meaning

Student A

1 <u>Underline</u> the correct verb form in each sentence (the -ing form or the to-infinitive). The first one has been done.

1 The clothes are still dirty because I forgot *switching* / <u>*to switch*</u> on the machine.
2 We regret *informing* / *to inform* you that we are not taking on any new staff at present.
3 I'm trying *running* / *to run* this computer program.
4 There's too much noise. Can you all stop *talking* / *to talk*, please?
5 I'm applying for a visa. It means *filling in* / *to fill* in this form.
6 First the teacher introduced herself, then she went on *explaining* / *to explain* about the course.
7 My shoes need *cleaning* / *to clean*.

2 Compare your answers with Student B. You should have <u>different</u> answers.

3 Now work together to check your answers by looking on page 152 of the book.

Lesson 13 Worksheet

Same verb, different meaning

Student B

1 <u>Underline</u> the correct verb form in each sentence (the -ing form or the to-infinitive). The first one has been done.

1 I'll never forget <u>*flying*</u> / *to fly* over the Grand Canyon. It was wonderful.
2 I regret *spending* / *to spend* all that money. I've got none left.
3 I tried *clicking* / *to click* on the box but it doesn't work. What can I try next?
4 An old man walking along the road stopped *talking* / *to talk* to us.
5 I think Nick meant *breaking* / *to break* that glass. It didn't look like an accident.
6 The teacher told everyone to be quiet but they just went on *talking* / *to talk*.
7 I need *cleaning* / *to clean* my shoes.

2 Compare your answers with Student A. You should have <u>different</u> answers.

3 Now work together to check your answers by looking on page 152 of the book.

At a glance

1 This lesson focuses on **noun grammar**. It contrasts:

- **plural and uncountable nouns without 'the'** (e.g. *cars*) to express general meaning
- **plural and uncountable nouns with 'the'** (e.g. *the cars*) to express specific meaning.

The lesson also presents some **special uses of 'the'** with nouns.

2 Exercises B and **C** in the book provide written controlled practice.

3 The **worksheet 'Education, sport, art and nature'** provides the students with an opportunity for further controlled and then freer, personalized spoken practice.

Lesson length

45 minutes

Preparation

- Photocopy one worksheet for every three students you have in the class. Cut the worksheet into the three parts.

Demonstration 1

1 Write the following words on the board:

> football
> curry
> chips
> mathematics
> parties
> snow
> museums

Put the students in pairs and give them a few minutes to discuss which things they like and don't like.

Get the students to report back on their conversations. You may notice that they are or are not using articles correctly at this point, but don't focus on the grammar yet.

Clarification 1

General and specific meanings (1, 2)

1 Ask students to think about the conversations they have just had. Ask: *Were you talking about specific examples of football, curry, mathematics, etc., or football, curry, mathematics etc. in general?* [in general].

2 Write these sentences on the board and highlight the nouns:

Uncountable noun	Plural noun
I don't like <u>curry</u>.	I like <u>chips</u>.

We can use a plural noun or an uncountable noun without **the** when we are talking about something in general.

3 Write these sentences on the board:

> I don't usually like <u>curry</u>, but I enjoyed <u>the curry</u> you gave me.
> I usually like <u>chips</u>, but I don't like <u>the chips</u> in that restaurant.

Ask: *Why do we use 'the' in the second part of each of these sentences?* [Because here the noun has a specific meaning, not a general meaning.] A phrase or clause like this after the noun often shows that it is specific.

5 However, sometimes a noun followed by a phrase or clause still has a general meaning. For example:

I hate <u>people who never smile</u>.
<u>Life in the old days</u> was hard.

6 A phrase with **of** usually takes **the**. For example:

a book on <u>Irish history</u>
a book on <u>the history of Ireland</u>.

Practice 1

Exercise B (individuals, pairs)

- Give the students five to ten minutes to complete Exercise B. Let them compare their answers in pairs before you check the correct answers with the whole class.

● Working in the same pairs, students can practise reading the conversations.

Demonstration 2

1 Write this sentence on the board. Ask the students whether they think it's true or false:

Tigers can swim.

[It's true.]

2 Ask the class: *How can you express this fact in a more formal way?* When the students are ready, write the answer on the board:

The tiger can swim.

Clarification 2

Special uses of the (3)

1 The second sentence about the tiger is one of a few special uses of **the**. Explain that we use **the** + singular noun to make general statements about animals, plants, inventions and discoveries:

The eucalyptus tree is common in Australia.
Who invented the camera?

We use this structure mainly in written English. In speech, 'Tigers can swim' is more usual.

2 We also use **the** with musical instruments: *She can play the guitar and the drums.*

Practice 2

Exercise C (pairs)

● Put the students in pairs to complete Exercise C as quickly as possible. Check the correct answers with the whole class.

Extra activity Worksheet (groups)
EDUCATION, SPORT, ART AND NATURE

● Divide the class into three groups, A, B and C. Give a copy of the Student A questionnaire to each student in Group A, the Student B questionnaire to each student in Group B, and so on. Give the groups a few minutes to underline the correct words in their questionnaires. Go round the class as the groups are working so that you can check that they all have the correct answers. [*Student A*: 1 maths, art 2 the grammar 3 history 4 the history 5 the sport 6 sport *Student B*: 1 films 2 the films 3 the piano, the violin 4 modern art 5 fashion 6 the colour *Student C*: 1 dogs, cats 2 wildlife 3 insects, spiders 4 the lakes and rivers 5 the eagle, the rose 6 people, animals]

● Reorganize the class into ABC groups and give them time to interview each other using their questionnaires.

● To close the lesson, invite students to report back on some interesting things that they found out about each other.

Lesson 14 Worksheet

Education, sport, art and nature

Student A: Education and sport

1 Underline the correct word(s) in each question.

1 What school subjects did (or do) you enjoy (*maths / the maths, art / the art,* etc.)?
2 Did you study *grammar / the grammar* of your own language at school?
3 Did you study *history / the history* at school?
4 How much do you know about *history / the history* of other countries?
5 Did (or Do) you enjoy *sport / the sport* that you did (or do) at school?
6 Do you prefer watching *sport / the sport* or playing it?

2 Now use the questions to interview other students.

Lesson 14 Worksheet

Education, sport, art and nature

Student B: The arts

1 Underline the correct word(s) in each question.

1 Do you like *films / the films*?
2 Do you prefer *films / the films* made in your country or US films?
3 Can you play a musical instrument (*piano / the piano, violin / the violin,* etc?)
4 Do you like *modern art / the modern art*? Why / Why not?
5 Are you interested in *fashion / the fashion*?
6 Do you like *colour / the colour* of the walls in the classroom? Why / why not?

2 Now use the questions to interview other students.

Lesson 14 Worksheet

Education, sport, art and nature

Student C: Nature

1 Underline the correct word(s) in each question.

1 Do you prefer *dogs / the dogs* or *cats / the cats*?
2 Are you interested in *wildlife / the wildlife* (for example birds and trees)?
3 Are you afraid of *insects / the insects* and *spiders / the spiders*?
4 Are *lakes and rivers / the lakes and rivers* in your country clean or polluted?
5 Does your country have a national plant or animal? (For example, *eagle / the eagle, rose / the rose*?)
6 Do you think *people / the people* are more intelligent than *animals / the animals*?

2 Now use the questions to interview other students.

15 Unit 89 Quite a, such a, what a, etc.

At a glance

1 This lesson clarifies different ways of **qualifying nouns**. It includes structures with:
- **quite a**, **such a** and **what a**
- **very**, **rather** and **quite**
- **so** and **such a**.

There is a focus on stress and intonation to express strength of feeling, so the lesson includes several drills.

2 **Exercise A** in the book gives controlled written practice in patterns with **very**, **quite**, **rather**, **so** and **such a**.

3 **Exercises B** and **C** in the book give controlled written practice of **so**, **such** and **so/such ... (that ...)**.

4 The lesson finishes with a **board game** on the **worksheet 'People, places, things and situations'**, which provides the opportunity for freer, personalized spoken practice.

Lesson length

60 minutes

Preparation

- Photocopy one worksheet for every three or four students in the class.
- Bring a dice for every three or four students in the class, and enough counters for everyone.

Demonstration 1

1 Draw these two symbols on the board, labelling them 'strong' and 'weak':

+++++	++
strong	weak

2 Read these groups of sentences to the class. (Don't write the sentences on the board at this stage.)

Ask the students to say whether the description in each group of sentences sounds strong or weak.

1 He's a man. He's a tall man. He's a fairly tall man.
2 She's a woman. She's a nice woman. What a woman!
3 It was a party. It was a really good party. It was quite a party!
4 It's an apple. It's a tasty apple. It's quite a tasty apple.
5 He's a fool. He's such a fool!
6 It's a book. It's an old book. It's rather an old book.
[1 weak 2 strong 3 strong 4 weak 5 strong 6 weak]

Clarification 1

Introduction (1, 4)

WHAT A ...

1 Ask: *What were the six nouns in the demonstration?* Write the nouns on the board:

man	apple
woman	fool
party	book

Point out that this lesson presents ways to show strong and weak opinions about things.

2 Write these sentences on the board and underline **what**, **quite** and **such**:

> <u>What</u> a woman!
> It was <u>quite</u> a party!
> He's <u>such</u> a fool!

3 After **quite**, **such** and **what** we can use a phrase with **a/an** to show that our opinion of the noun is strong. With **what** and **such** there is often an adjective as well. For example: *It's such a <u>small</u> house! What a <u>good</u> idea!*

Note: **quite** + **a/an** + adjective + noun has a different effect. See Clarification 2.

4 We use **what a/an** with a singular noun and **what** with a plural or uncountable noun. For example: *What lovely <u>flowers</u>! What <u>rubbish</u>!*

Practice 1

Extra activity (whole class)

REPETITION DRILL

- Get the students to listen to and repeat these sentences with the stress and intonation required to express a strong opinion. (All the underlined words should be stressed, but the main stress is on the word or syllables in capitals. The range 'up' and 'down' is quite wide.)

T: <u>What</u> a <u>WOman</u>!
SS: <u>What</u> a <u>WOman</u>!

T: It was <u>QUITE</u> a <u>party</u>!
SS: It was <u>QUITE</u> a <u>party</u>!

T: He's <u>such</u> a <u>FOOL</u>!
SS: He's <u>such</u> a <u>FOOL</u>!

T: It's <u>SUCH</u> a <u>nice</u> <u>HOUSE</u>!
SS: It's <u>SUCH</u> a <u>nice</u> <u>HOUSE</u>!

T: <u>What</u> a <u>good</u> <u>iDEa</u>!
SS: <u>What</u> a <u>good</u> <u>iDEa</u>!

T: <u>What</u> <u>LOVEly</u> <u>flowers</u>!
SS: <u>What</u> <u>LOVEly</u> <u>flowers</u>!

- Go through the drill a few times until the students are producing the sentences with appropriately expressive intonation.

Exercise D (pairs)

- Set this activity if you want to give your students extra practice in **what … .**

Demonstration 2

1 Ask the students if they can remember another 'strong' sentence about the party from the demonstration. Write this sentence on the board:

> +++++
>
> It was a really good party.

and add:

> It was a very good party.

2 Ask the students if they can remember the 'weak' sentences about the man, the apple and the book from the demonstration. Write the sentences on the board:

> ++
>
> He's a fairly tall man.
> It's quite a tasty apple.
> It's rather an old book.

Clarification 2

Very, quite, rather, etc. (2)

1 Underline **really**, **very** and **fairly** in the sentences on the board. Get the students to practise saying the sentences with sentence stress on these words.

Highlight the position of the adverbs of degree **really**, **very** and **fairly**:

a/an +	adverb +	adjective +	noun
It was a	really	good	party.
It was a	very	good	party.
He's a	fairly	tall	man.

2 In 'weak' sentences, **quite** goes before **a/an** + adjective + noun. Compare: *It was quite a party!* [strong] and *It was quite a good party.* [weak]

3 **Rather** can go in either position: *It's rather an old book.* OR *It's a rather old book.*

4 We can also use **very**, **quite**, **rather**, etc. + adjective + plural or uncountable noun. For example: *They're very old houses. This is quite nice coffee.*

* STUDENT SUPPORT For more information on adverbs of degree and **quite** and **rather**, refer students to Units 115 and 116.

Practice 2

Extra activity (whole class)
CHORAL DRILL

- Get the students to practise saying these sentences with the stress and intonation required to express a weak opinion. (All the underlined syllables should be stressed. The range 'up and down' is quite narrow or flat.)

T: He's a <u>fairly</u> <u>tall</u> man. SS: He's a <u>fairly</u> <u>tall</u> man.
T: It's <u>quite</u> a <u>tasty</u> apple. SS: It's <u>quite</u> a <u>tasty</u> apple.
T: It is <u>rather</u> an <u>old</u> book. SS: It is <u>rather</u> an <u>old</u> book.
T: They're <u>fairly</u> <u>old</u> houses. SS: They're <u>fairly</u> <u>old</u> houses.
T: This is <u>rather</u> nice coffee. S: This is <u>rather</u> nice coffee.

- Go through the drill a few times until the students are producing the sentences with appropriately cautious intonation.

Exercise A (individuals)

- Give the students five minutes to complete Exercise A. Let them compare their answers with a partner before you check the correct answers with the whole class. Encourage the students to use appropriately enthusiastic or cautious stress and intonation.

Exercise A Extension activity (whole class)
CUE/RESPONSE DRILL

- Get the students to 'disagree' with the sentences you say: they must give a weak opinion where yours is strong, and vice versa.

59

T: It's quite a good show. **very ...**
SS: It's a **very** good show!

T: She's a fairly tall woman. **really ...**
SS: She's a **really** tall woman!

T: It's a very grand hotel. **fairly ...**
SS: It's a **fairly** grand hotel.

T: It was quite a tiring journey. **very ...**
SS: It was a **very** tiring journey!

T: It's a really big flat. **quite ...**
SS: It's **quite** a big flat.

T: We had quite a nice meal. **really ...**
SS: We had a **really** nice meal!

Demonstration 3

1 Tell the students you had a really good holiday last year. Write these sentences on the board and ask the students if they can complete them in a very 'strong' way:

> It was s_____ _____ good holiday!
> The holiday was s_____ good!

When the students are ready, write the correct answers on the board:

> It was <u>such a</u> good holiday. The holiday was <u>so</u> good.

Leave the sentences on the board for Clarification 3.

Clarification 3

So and such a (3)

1 **So** and **such a/an** are used to express strong feelings.

2 Highlight the form:

> such a/an + adjective + noun
> It was <u>such a</u> good   holiday.
>
> so +   adjective
> The holiday was <u>so</u> good.

3 **So** can also be used with **long**, **far** and **many/much**, and **such** can be used with **a lot of**. For example: *It's <u>so long</u> since I last saw you. You waste <u>so much</u> time. There were <u>such a lot of</u> people.*

Practice 3

Exercise B (individuals, pairs)

• Give the students five minutes to do Exercise B, then check the answers with the whole class.

• Put the students in pairs to practise reading the conversation.

Demonstration 4

1 Write these three mixed-up sentences on the board and get the students to match them:

> Emma was so angry with Matthew that ... / ... she went to bed.
> She had such a bad headache that ... / ... she threw a plate at him.
> She was so happy that ... / ... she almost cried.

Write the correct answers on the board. Highlight the **so/such ... that** structure, and leave the sentences on the board for Clarification 4:

> Emma was <u>so angry</u> with Matthew <u>that</u> she threw a plate at him.
> She had <u>such a bad headache that</u> she went to bed.
> She was <u>so happy that</u> she almost cried.

Clarification 4

1 Ask the class: *What is the relationship between the first half and the second half of each sentence on the board?* [The second half of each sentence is the consequence of the first half of the sentence; the second event happened <u>because of</u> the first event.]

Practice 4

Exercise C (individuals, pairs)

• Give the students five to ten minutes to do Exercise C in the book, then check the answers with the whole class.

Extra activity Worksheet (small groups)
PEOPLE, PLACES, THINGS AND SITUATIONS
BOARD GAME

• Divide the class into groups of three or four. Give each group a copy of the worksheet game with a dice and counters. Give them a couple of minutes to read the instructions.
• Allow the class ten minutes or more to play the game. Go round the class as they are playing it to support and encourage. You could even join in yourself here and there.
• When most of the groups have finished, stop the game. Encourage the students to report to the rest of the class anything interesting that they found out about each other.

Lesson 15 Worksheet

People, places, things and situations

Instructions

1 Play the game in groups of three or four.
2 Place your counters on START.
3 Roll the dice. Move forward the number of spaces shown on the dice.
4 Read the sentence in the square. Have you ever thought it? Have you ever said it? Tell your group about the place, person, thing or situation.
6 If you can't think of anything to say, you miss a turn in the next round.
7 The first person to reach FINISH is the winner.

START	PERSON She is a very intelligent person.	SITUATION This is taking so much longer than I planned!	THING They're a rather old pair of jeans, but I don't want to throw them away.
SITUATION I'm so happy that I want to dance.	PLACE This hill is so steep I don't think I can go any further.	PERSON He's such an idiot.	PLACE What beautiful buildings!
PLACE It's so cold that you can't stay outdoors for long.	PERSON She's got such a lovely smile.	SITUATION I feel so embarrassed that I want to disappear!	SITUATION I'm so worried about it that I can't sleep at night.
PLACE or THING It was rather a disappointment.	PERSON What a tall man!	PLACE I'd like to go there more often but it's such a long way from here.	PLACE The food there was so awful that I couldn't eat it.
PLACE I'd like to go there more often but it's so expensive.	PERSON It's such a long time since I've seen him.	PLACE There were so many people there I could hardly move.	SITUATION I felt so ill that I had to stay in bed all day.
SITUATION What rubbish he's talking!	SITUATION I find it really annoying.	THING It's so important to me that I always take it on holiday with me.	PERSON He's got quite a long beard.
THING It's so valuable that I worry about breaking it or losing it.	THING It's very old and worth quite a lot of money.	SITUATION I'm so angry that I can't speak!	FINISH

16 Unit 95 A lot of, lots of, many, much, (a) few and (a) little

At a glance

1 This lesson reviews **quantifiers** including **a lot of, lots of, many, much, (a) few** and **(a) little**.

2 **Exercise A** in the book gives controlled written practice of **a lot of, lots of, many, much, a few** and **a little**.

3 **'Places to visit'** on the **worksheet** and **Exercise D** in the book give further controlled practice within the context of describing places.

4 **'Where is it?'** on the **worksheet** provides the students with an opportunity for freer written practice with a communicative outcome.

Lesson length

50 minutes

Preparation

- Copy the sentences for the demonstration on to an OHT if you plan to use the OHP.
- Make one copy of the worksheet for each student in the class.

Demonstration

1 Write the following sentences on the board or project them on an OHP:

> A It gets lots of snow.
> B There are a lot of interesting animals there.
> C It doesn't get much rain.
> D There aren't many old buildings there.

Put the students in pairs for a minute or two to discuss which places in their country or in the world these sentences could describe, then discuss the answers with the whole class. Leave the sentences on the board for Clarification 1.

Clarification 1

Introduction – talking about quantities (1)

1 Underline the quantifiers in the sentences on the board:

> A It gets <u>lots of</u> snow.
> B There are <u>a lot of</u> interesting animals there.
> C It doesn't get <u>much</u> rain.
> D There aren't <u>many</u> old buildings there.

A lot of, lots of, many and **much** all mean a <u>large</u> quantity.

2 Highlight **not much/many** in Sentences C and D:

> C It does<u>n't</u> get <u>much</u> rain.
> D There are<u>n't</u> <u>many</u> old buildings there.

Ask the class if they can express the meaning of these two sentences in another way. When the students are ready, write these two sentences on the board and underline the quantifiers:

> C It only gets <u>a little</u> rain.
> D There are <u>a few</u> old buildings there.

A few and **a little** mean a <u>small</u> quantity.

3 Ask the class: *What kind of nouns are 'animals' and 'old buildings'?* [Plural nouns.] *What kind of nouns are 'snow' and 'rain'?* [Uncountable nouns.] Highlight the forms:

> many, a few + plural noun
> much, a little + uncountable noun

4 Point out that **a lot of** and **lots of** can go before both plural nouns and uncountable nouns, e.g.: *a lot of interesting plants, a lot of rain, lots of old buildings, lots of snow.* Add this to the information on the board:

> many, a few + plural noun
> lots of, a lot of
>
> much, a little + uncountable noun
> lots of, a lot of

5 We can use all these quantifiers without a noun if it is clear what we mean: *It gets some rain, but not as <u>much</u> as it did before. Twenty years ago it got <u>a lot</u>.*

Note: In this case we say **a lot** without **of**.

Practice 1

Exercise A (individuals)

● Give the students about five minutes to complete Exercise A. Let them compare their answers in pairs, then check the correct answers with the whole class.

Clarification 2

A lot of, many and much (2)

1 As a general rule, we use **a lot of** and **lots of** in positive statements and **many** and **much** in negatives and questions.

+ *There are <u>lots of</u> / <u>a lot of</u> interesting animals there. There <u>aren't many</u> old buildings. It <u>doesn't get</u> much rain.*
? *<u>How much</u> snow does it get? <u>How many</u> old buildings are there?*

2 We can use **many** and **much** after **too**, **so** and **as**.

There's <u>too much</u> rain.
There are <u>so many</u> old buildings!
It doesn't get <u>as much</u> snow as before.

3 In formal English, we can sometimes use **much** and **many** in a positive statement. For example: *<u>Many</u> people visit this city. There is <u>much</u> interest in the development of the old part of the city.*

This is less usual in conversation, where we normally use **a lot of** and **lots of**.

4 In informal English you may hear **a lot of** in a negative or a question. For example: *It doesn't get <u>a lot of</u> snow. There aren't <u>a lot of</u> old buildings.*

Extra activity (whole class)
FORMAL/INFORMAL TRANSFORMATION DRILL

1 Use this quick transformation drill to break up the clarification and to give the students some very controlled oral practice. Tell the students you are going to say formal or neutral sentences; they need to transform them into informal sentences.

T: Many people like him.
SS: A lot of people like him.

T: Do you eat much fruit?
SS: Do you eat a lot of fruit?

T: Have you got many books?
SS: Have you got a lot of books?

T: There is much demand for it.
SS: There's a lot of demand for it.

Repeat the drill a few times until the students are producing the sentences comfortably.

Now, you're going to say informal sentences and this time the students need to transform them into formal or neutral sentences.

T: A lot of people work here.
SS: Many people work here.

T: Do you drink a lot of water?
SS: Do you drink much water?

T: Have you got a lot of friends?
SS: Have you got many friends?

T: There's a lot of interest in it.
SS: There's much interest in it.

Again, repeat the drill a few times.

Few and a little with and without a (3)

1 Compare these sentences with the class:

A *I've made <u>few</u> good friends here.*
B *I've made <u>a few</u> good friends here.*

Ask: *Is Speaker A happy?* [No – 'few' describes a small quantity with a negative meaning.] *Is Speaker B happy?* [Yes – 'a few' describes a small quantity with a positive meaning.]

2 Compare these sentences with the class:

A *I've made <u>little</u> progress with the language.*
B *I've made <u>a little</u> progress with the language.*

Ask: *Is Speaker A happy with their progress?* [No – 'little' describes a small quantity with a negative meaning.] *Is Speaker B happy?* [Yes – 'a little' describes a small quantity with a positive meaning.]

3 Highlight the forms:

> few, a few + plural noun
> little, a little + uncountable noun

4 **Few** and **little** without **a** can be rather formal. In informal speech we can use these structures:

I have<u>n't</u> made <u>many</u> good friends here.
I've have<u>n't</u> made <u>much</u> progress with the language.

Practice 2

Worksheet (individuals)
PLACES TO VISIT – EXERCISES 1 AND 2

● Give a worksheet to each student in the class. Direct them to Exercise 1 on the worksheet and Exercise D in the book. Give them one minute to read the two texts and answer the question. Get a show of hands for those who would prefer each place for a holiday. Ask a few students to give their reasons.

- Give the students a few minutes to do Exercise 2. Let them compare their answers in pairs, then check the correct answers with the whole class [1 a few 2 little 3 much 4 few 5 many 6 a few 7 many].

Exercise D (individuals)

- Give the students about five minutes to complete Exercise D. Let them compare their answers in pairs, then check the correct answers with the whole class.

Extra activity Worksheet (individuals, groups)
WHERE IS IT?

- Direct the students to Exercise 3 on the worksheet. Tell them to think about a place they know, either in their own country or in another country. They are going to write a paragraph about it using language from the lesson and ideas from the worksheet, but they mustn't include the name of the place they are writing about in their paragraph. Other students are going to read their paragraph and guess where the place is.

- Allow the students about ten minutes to write their paragraphs. Go round the class as the students are working so that you can check their work and give help as necessary.

- When all the students are ready, put them into groups of five or six. Get them to read each other's work and to see if they know which places are being described.

Exercises B and C

- Exercises B and C could be set for homework.

Lesson 16 Worksheet

Places to visit

1 Quickly read this paragraph and Exercise D in the book. Which place would you choose for a holiday? Why?

The city centre is a busy and exciting place. There are *much / a lot of* excellent shops and bars, and (1) *few / a few* good museums and galleries too. There is (2) *little / a little* crime here, so tourists can feel safe even at night. There isn't as (3) *many / much* sightseeing to do as in other big cities, however there are some interesting old buildings to see. Unfortunately, the city is very polluted and there are too (4) *few / a few* green spaces. There aren't (5) *many / much* trees or flowers, for example. However, there are (6) *few / a few* small parks where children can play. There are so (7) *much / many* good restaurants you'll find it hard to choose where to eat!

2 Underline the correct words.

Where is it?

3 Write a paragraph about a place you know, either in your own country or abroad. Don't say the name of the place! Include information about some of these things using **much**, **many**, **a few**, **little**, etc:

> shops   bars   cafés   museums   crime   old buildings   pollution
> trees and flowers   green spaces   parks where children can play
> money   tourists   contact between local people and the outside world
> bicycles   cars   entertainment

....

....

....

....

....

....

....

....

....

....

17 Unit 100 Reflexive pronouns

At a glance

1 The lesson focuses on the use of **reflexive pronouns**:
- when the object of the sentence is the same as the subject
- after certain prepositions.

2 **Exercises A** and **B** in the book give controlled practice of reflexive pronouns when the subject is the same as the object.

3 **Exercise C** gives controlled practice of reflexive pronouns after certain prepositions.

4 The **worksheet 'Find someone who …'** provides the opportunity for freer, personalized spoken and written practice of reflexive pronouns.

Lesson length

45–60 minutes

Preparation

- Photocopy one worksheet for every three students you have in the class. Cut the worksheet into the three parts.

Demonstration

1 Mime handling a camera: pick it up, switch it on, take a photo of yourself and put it down again near you. (Alternatively, use a real camera or camera phone.)

Write these sentences on the board and ask the students to complete them:

> I've got my camera with _____ today.
> I've just taken a photo of _____ with it.

When the students are ready, add the missing words to the sentence.

> I've got my camera with <u>me</u> today.
> I've just taken a photo of <u>myself</u> with it.

Leave the sentences on the board for Clarification 1.

Clarification 1

The form and use of reflexive pronouns (1, 2, 3)

1 Ask the class: *What kind of word is 'me'?* [A pronoun; an object pronoun to be precise.] *What kind of word is 'I'?* [A pronoun; a subject pronoun to be precise.]

* STUDENT SUPPORT For more information on subject and object pronouns, direct the students to Unit 98.2.

2 Ask: *What kind of word is 'myself'?* [A reflexive pronoun. It refers back to the subject, 'I'.] Check that students know how to form all the reflexive pronouns. Write these subject pronouns on the board:

> I –
> he –
> she –
> it –
> you (singular) –
> we –
> you (plural) –
> they –

Invite students to come up and add the reflexive pronouns:

> I – myself
> he – himself
> she – herself
> it – itself
> you (singular) – yourself
> we – ourselves
> you (plural) – yourselves
> they – themselves

3 Give the class some more examples of how reflexive pronouns are used: *Mark made <u>himself</u> a sandwich. We've locked <u>ourselves</u> out.*

4 To check the students' understanding, write these two sentences on the board:

> A When the policeman came in, the gunman shot <u>him</u>.
> B When the policeman came in, the gunman shot <u>himself</u>.

Ask: *In A, who did the gunman shoot?* [The policeman.] *In B, who did the gunman shoot?* [The gunman.]

Practice 1

Exercise A (pairs)

- Put the students in pairs and give them a few minutes to complete Exercise A. Then check the correct answers with the whole class.

Exercise B (individuals)

- Give the students a few minutes to complete Exercise B. Let them compare their answers in pairs, then check the correct answers with the whole class.

Exercise B Extension activity (whole class)
CUE/RESPONSE DRILL

- Use this drill based on Exercise B to give the students very controlled oral practice. Books closed.

T: Shall I get the tickets? **It's OK …**
SS: It's OK, I can pay for myself.

T: I've got lots of photos of my children. **Yes, but …**
SS: Yes, but you haven't got many of yourself.

T: Did you have a good time? **No, we …**
SS: No, we had to amuse ourselves.

T: Why has the light gone off? **It …**
SS: It switches itself off automatically.

Clarification 2

Reflexive pronouns after a preposition (3)

1 Reflexive pronouns can be used after prepositions. For example: *He's only interested in himself. She often talks to herself.*

2 However, when the preposition gives information about location, we use **me, you, him,** etc. For example: *I've got my camera with me. She saw a man in front of her.*

Practice 2

Exercise C (individuals)

- Give the students a few minutes to complete Exercise C. Let them compare their answers in pairs, then check the correct answers with the whole class.

Extra activity (groups)
FIND SOMEONE WHO …

- Write this example on the board:

> Find someone who has hurt himself or herself recently.

- Ask the class: *What question do you need to ask to find this information?* Write on the board:

> Have you hurt yourself recently?

- Put the question to the class. If someone says 'yes', write their name on the board and find out more information about the incident. Write a summarizing sentence or two on the board. The sentences should include a reflexive pronoun. For example:

> Coralie and Arnold have hurt themselves recently.
> Coralie cut herself when she was cooking last week.
> Arnold hurt himself when he was playing tennis.

- Hand out one set of the 'Find someone who …' questions from the worksheet to each student in the class (i.e. three questions each). Give the students a few minutes to prepare the questions that they need to ask.
- Put the students into large groups to ask each other their questions. Make sure they note down people's names and any extra information they find out. Encourage them to find out more than one name if possible.
- After about ten minutes, get the students to write some summarizing sentences about what they found out about each other. They can also write about themselves.
- To bring the activity to a close, ask students to read out their most interesting sentences to the whole class.

Extra clarification

Idioms with reflexive pronouns; verbs without a reflexive pronoun (4, 5)

1 Point out to the students that there are some everyday idioms with reflexive pronouns. Ask the class if they know any. Give a few examples:

Enjoy yourselves! (= Have a good time.)
Help yourself! (= Take as many/much as you want.)
Make yourself at home. (= Be relaxed and comfortable.)

There are more examples on page 236.

2 Some English verbs do not usually take a reflexive pronoun, although they may in other languages. These verbs include: **hurry, meet, feel** + adjective, **relax, concentrate, get out, wake up.**

There are more examples on page 236.

3 We do not normally use a reflexive pronoun with
change (clothes), **dress**, and **wash**. But we can use
a reflexive pronoun when the action is difficult.
For example: *A friend is disabled, but she can dress
<u>herself</u>.*

Note: Idioms with reflexive pronouns and verbs
without a reflexive pronoun aren't focused on in this
lesson plan. However, if you choose to include this
focus in your lesson, Exercise D provides controlled
practice.

Lesson 17 Worksheet

Find someone who …

Find someone who has taught himself or herself to do something.

Have you ever……………………………………………………..………?

Name (s):

Find someone who can make himself or herself cry.

Can you……………………………………………..…………..……?

Name (s):

Find someone who looks at himself or herself in the mirror less than three times a day.

How often……………………………………..………………..………?

Name (s):

Find someone who finds it easy to laugh at himself or herself.

Do you……..…………………………………………….…………?

Name (s):

Find someone who has photographed himself or herself recently.

Have you …………………………………………………..…...?

Name (s):

Find someone who finds it easy to introduce himself or herself to new people.

Do you……………………………………………………?

Name (s):

Find someone who has seen himself/herself on TV or heard himself/herself on the radio.

Have you ever…………………………………………………?

Name (s):

Find someone who never cooks dinner for himself or herself in the evening.

Do you……………………………………………..…………?

Name (s):

Find someone who sometimes talks to himself or herself.

Do you sometimes…………………………………………………?

Name (s):

18 Unit 107 Interesting and interested

Lesson length

50 minutes

Preparation

- Photocopy one worksheet for each pair of students. Cut the worksheets in half.

Demonstration

1 Tell the class you are going to test their memories! You are going to give them some information about three friends of yours, Ian, Fay and Tom. They need to remember it. Write the three names on the board, then say these sentences twice to the class:

Ian is interested in ice skating.
Fay is fascinated by France.
Tom is terrified of tarantulas.

Put the students in pairs. Ask the students what they can remember about the three people, and ask for answers from the whole class after about a minute.

Leave the three sentences on the board for the clarification.

Clarification

Introduction (1, 2)

ADJECTIVE PAIRS

1 Write the three sentences on the board. Underline the -ed adjective in each sentence.

> Ian is <u>interested</u> in ice skating.
> Fay is <u>fascinated</u> by France.
> Tom is <u>terrified</u> of tarantulas.

2 Write these gapped sentences on the board and ask the students what they think the missing words are:

> Ian: 'I think ice skating is _____.'
> Fay: 'I think France is _____.'
> Tom: 'I think tarantulas are _____.'

Write the correct answers on the board:

> Ian: 'I think ice skating is <u>interesting</u>.'
> Fay: 'I think France is <u>fascinating</u>.'
> Tom: 'I think tarantulas are <u>terrifying</u>.'

3 Ask the class: *Which adjectives focus on the person's feelings, the -ing adjectives or the -ed adjectives?* [The -ed adjectives.] *What do the -ing adjectives focus on in these sentences?* [Ice skating, France and tarantulas.]

4 Point out that there are many other adjective pairs like these ones, and ask the students if they can call out any more.

* STUDENT SUPPORT Many -ed adjectives are followed by prepositions, e.g. **interested in**, **fascinated by**. For more information on this, refer the students to Unit 125.2.

Practice

Exercise A (pairs)

- Put the students in pairs and give them a couple of minutes to complete Exercise A.
- Check the correct answers with the whole class. As you do so, make sure the students can pronounce the -ed endings correctly: /ɪd/ and /aɪd/.

Exercise A Extension activity (whole class)
PICTURE PROMPT DRILL

- Extend Exercise A with this picture prompt drill. Tell the students to cover page 253 so that only the five pictures at the top of the page show. Tell them that you want them to say how each person feels.

T: Example picture: **He's ...**
SS: ...depressed.

T: Picture 1: **He's ...**
SS: ...exhausted.

T: Picture 2: **She's ...**
SS: ...interested.

T: Picture 3: **He's ...**
SS: ...fascinated.

T: Picture 4: **She's ...**
SS: ...excited.

- Now tell them you want to finish these sentences:
  T: The place is ...
  SS: ...depressing.

  T: His day was ...
  SS: ...exhausting.

  T: Astronomy is ...
  SS: ...interesting.

  T: Chess is ...
  SS: ...fascinating.

  T: The news is ...
  SS: ...exciting.

- Monitor and correct the students' pronunciation. Repeat the drills through a few times until the students are producing the adjectives comfortably.

- Finally, mix the -ed and -ing adjective answers in the drill. E.g.:

  T: He's ...
  SS: ...depressed.

  T: The place is ...
  SS: ...depressing.

  T: His day was ...
  SS: ...exhausting.

  T: He's ...
  SS: ...exhausted,

  and so on.

Extra activity Worksheet (pairs)
ADJECTIVE PAIRS

- Students must have their books closed for Stages 1 and 2 of this activity.
- Divide the class into two groups, Group A and Group B. Student As should work together in AA pairs and Student Bs in BB pairs. Show the worksheets and give the instruction to underline the correct adjective in each sentence. Give a Student A worksheet to all the students in Group A and a Student B worksheet to all the students in Group B, and give the students five to ten minutes to complete them.

- Reorganize the students into AB pairs and tell them to read out their sentences to each other. They should have different adjective answers for each item. If they have the same adjective answers, then one of them is wrong. In this case, they need to look at their sentences together to see which answer needs to be changed.

- When they have finished comparing their sentences they can open their books to check their answers on page 252.

Exercise B (individuals, pairs)

- Direct the students to Exercise B in the book. Give them five minutes to complete the exercise. Let the students compare their answers in pairs before you check the correct answers with the whole class.

- Put the students in pairs again to practise reading the dialogue with their partner a few times.

Extra activity Worksheet (small groups)
TALK ABOUT ...

- Direct the students to 'Talk about ...' at the bottom of the worksheet. Give them a few minutes to look at the questions and think about their answers. Then put the students into small groups to talk about the questions.

- At the end of the activity, invite groups to report back on whether their answers were similar or different.

Exercise C

- Exercise C could be set for homework.

Lesson 18 Worksheet

Adjective pairs

Student A

1 <u>Underline</u> the correct adjective in each sentence.

1 Tom told us an *amused / amusing* story.
2 The two-hour delay was *annoyed / annoying*.
3 I went to the party but I felt *bored / boring*.
4 This computer has some very *confused / confusing* instructions.
5 This weather makes me so *depressed / depressing*.
6 I was very *disappointed / disappointing* not to get the job.
7 The United fans were *excited / exciting*.
8 Going for a jog with Matthew is *exhausted / exhausting*.
9 I watched the programme on wildlife. I was absolutely *fascinated / fascinating*.
10 For one *frightened / frightening* moment I thought I was going to fall.
11 I don't understand. I find the whole thing rather *puzzled / puzzling*.
12 Lying in a hot bath is *relaxed / relaxing*.
13 I think the way Jessica behaved was quite *shocked / shocking*.
14 I was *surprised / surprising* at the test results.
15 We were *thrilled / thrilling* to hear your good news.
16 After travelling all day and night they were *tired / tiring*.

2 Compare your answers with Student B. You should have <u>different</u> answers.

3 Now work together to check your answers by looking at page 252 of the book.

Talk about …

- what you do when you're **bored** on a long journey
- an **exciting** film you've seen
- something you find **frightening**
- another country and culture that you are **interested** in
- the last time you got really **annoyed** with someone or something
- a TV programme you find **amusing**
- what kind of weather makes you **depressed**
- something you find **confusing** in English grammar.

Lesson 18 Worksheet

Adjective pairs

Student B

1 <u>Underline</u> the correct adjective in each sentence.

1 We were *amused / amusing* at Tom's story.
2 The passengers were *annoyed / annoying* about the delay.
3 I didn't enjoy the party. It was *bored / boring*.
4 I got very *confused / confusing* trying to make sense of the instructions.
5 This wet weather is so *depressed / depressing*.
6 It was very *disappointed / disappointing* not to get the job.
7 The game was really *exciting / excited*.
8 I'm *exhausted / exhausting* after jogging all that way.
9 I thought the programme on wildlife was *fascinated / fascinating*.
10 When I got on to the roof I felt *frightened / frightening*.
11 I must say, I'm *puzzled / puzzling*. I just don't understand.
12 I feel *relaxed / relaxing* when I lie in a hot bath.
13 I was quite *shocked / shocking* to see Jessica behaving like that.
14 The test results were *surprised / surprising*.
15 What *thrilled / thrilling* news this is! Congratulations!
16 The journey took all day and all night. They found it very *tired / tiring*.

2 Compare your answers with Student A. You should have <u>different</u> answers.

3 Now work together to check your answers by looking at page 252 of the book.

Talk about …

- what you do when you're **bored** on a long journey
- an **exciting** film you've seen
- something you find **frightening**
- another country and culture that you are **interested** in
- the last time you got really **annoyed** with someone or something
- a TV programme you find **amusing**
- what kind of weather makes you **depressed**
- something you find **confusing** in English grammar.

19 Unit 122 During or while?
By or until? As or like?

At a glance

1 This lesson focuses on **link words** and **prepositions** including:
- **during** and **while** to talk about things happening at the same time
- **by** and **until** to talk about things happening before a time
- **as**, **like** and **as if / as though** to talk about function and similarity.

2 The **worksheet 'Place your Bets'** is a fun test of the students' knowledge of the link words and prepositions.

3 Exercises **A** to **E** in the book provide controlled written practice.

4 The **extra activity 'Speaking'** gives the students an opportunity for personalized practice of some of the link words and prepositions.

Lesson length

45–60 minutes

Preparation

- Make one copy of the worksheet for each student in the class.
- Copy the sentences for the extra activity on to an OHT if you plan to use the OHP.

Demonstration

Worksheet (teams)

PLACE YOUR BETS

1 Divide the class into teams (pairs or small groups). Give one copy of the worksheet to each student. Make sure all the students have their books closed.

Give the teams five to ten minutes to read the nine sentences and together choose the correct ending for each one. The teams also need to place a bet on each of their answers at this point: if they are completely sure they have chosen the correct ending, they can bet 100 points; if they are less sure they can bet between 10 and 90 points.

2 Go through the answers one by one during the clarification stage. As you do this, the teams should keep a record of the points they win and lose. (If they made a correct choice and bet 60 points, for example, they win 60 points. If they made an incorrect choice and bet 60 points, they lose 60 points.)

Clarification 1

During or while? (1)

1 Ask the teams to say what they think is the correct ending for Sentence 1 on the worksheet [1b].

Write the sentence on the board and underline **during**:

> The phone rang <u>during</u> the meal.

Ask: *Did the phone ring before, after, or in the middle of the meal?* [In the middle of the meal.] *What kind of word is 'during'?* [A preposition, like **in**.]

During comes before a noun (e.g. *the lesson*). Make sure students can pronounce **during** correctly: /ˈdjʊərɪŋ/.

2 Ask the students: *How could you change Sentence 1a to make it correct?* [The phone rang <u>while</u> (or <u>when</u>) we were eating.]

While is a linking word (like **when**). It comes before a clause (e.g. *… while they were asleep*). Ask: *Does 'during the meal' mean the same as 'while we were eating'?* [Yes.]

By or until? (2)

1 Ask the teams to say what they think the correct endings for Sentences 2, 3 and 4 are. [2b 3a 4b]

Write Sentence 2 on the board and underline **until**:

> I'm working <u>until</u> Thursday.

2 Ask students to suggest other ways that this sentence could finish. [*I'm working until 10 o'clock, the end of the month, next summer, etc.*]

Until means 'from one time up to another time'. (Note: **Till** means the same as **until**, but is more informal.)

3 Write Sentence 3 on the board and underline **by**:

> They hope to finish the new bridge <u>by</u> next July.

Draw these two timelines on the board and ask the students to say which one represents Sentence 3:

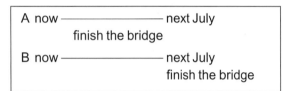

[Timeline A.]

Ask students to suggest other ways that this sentence could finish. [*They hope to finish the new bridge by the end of the month, 2020, etc.*]

By means 'at some time before another time'.

4 Write Sentence 4 on the board, underlining **by the time**:

> The party was over <u>by the time</u> we arrived.

Ask students: *When did the party finish?* [Before we arrived.] Ask students to suggest other ways that this sentence could finish. [*The party was over by the time the police arrived, I phoned you, etc.*]

We use **by the time** before a clause. We can also use **until** before a clause. For example: *There was no food left <u>by the time we arrived</u>. I'll wait <u>until you're ready</u>.*

* STUDENT SUPPORT For more information on the Present Simple after **until** etc. see Unit 27.2.

Practice 1

● The lesson so far has focused on link words and prepositions related to time. Check how many points the teams have won and lost so far. Then set Exercises A and B in the book.

Exercise A (pairs)

● Put the students in pairs and give them three to five minutes to complete Exercise A. Then check the correct answers with the whole class.

Exercise B (pairs)

● Keep the students in pairs and give them three to five minutes to complete Exercise B. Then check the correct answers with the whole class.

Clarification 2

As, like, and as if / as though (3)

1 Ask the teams to say what they think the correct endings for Sentences 5 and 6 are. [5a 6b]

Write Sentences 5 and 6 on the board and underline **as** and **like**:

> Kevin works <u>as</u> a manager.
> Lucia's very intelligent but she talks <u>like</u> a child.

Ask: *Is Kevin a manager?* [Yes.] *Is Lucia a child?* [No.] We use **as** to talk about a job or function. We use **like** to talk about things being similar.

2 Highlight the form in these two sentences:

> **as** + noun   **like** + noun

3 Ask the teams to say what they think the correct endings for Sentences 7 and 8 are. [7b 8a]

Write Sentences 7 and 8 on the board and underline **as though** and **as**:

> Frank looks <u>as though</u> he's tired.
> John and Sue are having a summer party, <u>as</u> they did last year.

Ask: *Is Frank definitely tired?* [No – he <u>seems</u> tired.] *Did John and Sue definitely have a summer party last year?* [Yes.]

4 Highlight the form in these two sentences:

> **as though** + clause   **as** + clause

In these sentences, **as though** can be replaced by **as if**, and **as** can be replaced by **like**. **Like** is more informal than **as**.

5 Ask the teams to say what they think the correct ending for Sentence 9 is. [9b]

Write Sentence 9 on the board and underline **as**:

> I haven't got much money, <u>as</u> you know.

We use **as** with verbs of speaking and knowing, e.g. *as I told you …, as you expected … .*

6 At this point, find out which team won the most points and won the game on the worksheet. Make sure everyone in the class now has a correctly completed worksheet for their records.

Practice 2

Exercise C (pairs)

- Put the students in pairs and give them three to five minutes to complete Exercise C. Then check the correct answers with the whole class.

Exercise D (pairs)

- Keep the students in pairs and give them three to five minutes to complete Exercise D. Then check the correct answers with the whole class.

Exercise E (pairs)

- Keep the students in pairs and give them three to five minutes to complete Exercise E. Then check the correct answers with the whole class.

Extra activity (pairs)

SPEAKING

- Write the following gapped questions on the board or project them on an OHP:

> 1 How many times do you usually wake up _____ the night?
> 2 Do you ever watch TV _____ you're eating a meal?
> 3 Are you usually in bed _____ midnight?
> 4 Have you ever worked _____ a waiter?
> 5 Does it look _____ it's going to rain today?
> 6 Do you think you look _____ someone famous?

- Put the students in pairs to complete each question with a word or phrase from the lesson. Go through the correct answers with the whole class. [1 during 2 while/when 3 by 4 as 5 as if/though 6 like]
- Put the students into different pairs to interview each other, using the questions. After about five minutes, invite students to report back on what they found out about each other.

Lesson 19 Worksheet

Place your bets

Look at the sentences below. Tick ✓ the correct ending for each sentence. How sure are you about your choice? Bet between 10 and 100 points.

1 The phone rang during
   a) we were eating. ......
   b) the meal. ......
   Bet 1 ......

2 I'm working
   a) by Thursday. ......
   b) until Thursday. ......
   Bet 2 ......

3 They hope to finish the new bridge
   a) by next July. ......
   b) until next July. ......
   Bet 3 ......

4 The party was over by
   a) when we arrived. ......
   b) the time we arrived. ......
   Bet 4 ......

5 Kevin works as
   a) a manager. ......
   b) if a manager. ......
   Bet 5 ......

6 Lucia's very intelligent but she talks
   a) as a child. ......
   b) like a child. ......
   Bet 6 ......

7 Frank looks as
   a) tired. ......
   b) though he's tired. ......
   Bet 7 ......

8 John and Sue are having a summer party, as
   a) they did last year.
   b) if they did last year.
   Bet 8 ......

9 I haven't got much money,
   a) like you know. ....
   b) as you know. ....
   Bet 9 ......

Points won:	Points lost:
Total:	

At a glance

1 This lesson focuses on the **meaning of the adverbs down**, **off**, **on**, **out**, **over** and **up** in **phrasal verbs**.

2 Using the **worksheet 'Phrasal verbs – adverb meanings'**, each student initially focuses on just one or two adverb meanings. The students then work in groups to share their knowledge and to complete **Exercise A** in the book.

3 **Exercises B** and **C** in the book provide further controlled practice of some of the phrasal verbs in context.

4 The **extra activity 'Speaking'** provides the opportunity for freer, personalized spoken practice of some of the phrasal verbs from the lesson.

Lesson length

45–60 minutes

Preparation

- Make a copy of the worksheet for each student in the class.
- Copy the questions for the final extra activity on to an OHT if you plan to use the OHP.

Demonstration

1 Switch the lights off in your classroom. Ask a student to go and switch the lights on.

Ask the class: *Shall I leave the lights on or switch them off?*

Clarification

Adverb meanings (2)

1 Write the phrasal verbs from the demonstration on the board and underline the adverbs:

> Switch the lights <u>on</u>. / Switch the lights <u>off</u>.
> Leave the lights <u>on</u>.

2 Ask the students what **on** and **off** mean in this context ['connected' and 'disconnected']. Ask if they can think of other phrasal verbs with **on** and **off**, where the adverbs **on** and **off** have this meaning. [E.g. **turn on/off**.]

3 Tell the students that the adverbs in phrasal verbs carry a lot of the meaning. Knowing the most common adverb meanings will help students to understand new phrasal verbs when they meet them. With books closed, ask the students to call out what

they think are the most common adverbs in phrasal verbs [**down**, **off**, **on**, **out**, **over**, **up**].

Practice

Extra activity Worksheet (groups)

ADVERB EXPERTS

- Divide the class into four groups, A, B, C and D. Tell the class that each group is going to become an expert on the meanings of one or two adverbs commonly found in phrasal verbs. Hand out a copy of the worksheet to each student, but make sure that each group only focuses on their section (A, B, C or D) of the worksheet at this stage.
- Direct the students to the list of adverb meanings and example phrasal verbs on page 312. Tell each group to complete their part of the worksheet by writing the correct adverb meanings and example sentences from page 312 in the table. They are now 'experts' on those adverb meanings. As an example, Group A's worksheets at this stage should look like this:

A Phrasal verbs with **down**

Adverb	**down**			
Meaning	becoming less	**completely to the ground**	stopping completely	**on paper**
Example phrasal verbs	turn down the music bring down the cost of living	knock a house down cut down a tree	the car broke down a factory closing down	copy down the words write down the message note down the details

Extra activity (groups)

PREPARATION FOR EXERCISE A

- Now tell the class to look at Exercise A. The phrasal verbs in this exercise are different from the ones they have just been looking at, but the adverb meanings are the same. They should look through Exercise A quickly and find the phrasal verb adverbs that they are 'experts' on. They must decide which meaning the adverbs in those phrasal verbs have. They should then write those new phrasal verbs into the relevant column on their worksheets.
- Group A's worksheets at this stage should now look like this:

A Phrasal verbs with **down**

Adverb	**down**			
Meaning	becoming less	**completely to the ground**	stopping completely	**on paper**
Example phrasal verbs	turn down the music bring down the cost of living keep its costs down	knock a house down cut down a tree burnt down by terrorists	the car broke down a factory closing down many firms have shut down	copy down the words write down the message note down the details get these ideas down

Extra activity Exercise A (groups)

- Reorganize the class into ABCD groups. Tell the students to do Exercise A by working together as a group and sharing their expert knowledge with each other.
  Note: If you have a small class, you could divide the students into just two 'expert' groups, Group A and Group B. Group A work on worksheet Sections A and B and Group B work on Sections C and D. The students then work in AB pairs at this stage.
- Go through the correct answers with the whole class.

Exercise B (individuals, pairs)

- Give the students five minutes to do the exercise individually. With weaker classes you could write the adverbs needed on the board, but in the wrong order.

down	out
on	out
on	out
off	out

- Let students compare their answers in pairs before you check with the whole class.
- Put the students in pairs to practise reading the conversations.

Extra activity (whole class)
TRANSFORMATION DRILL

- Give the students very controlled oral practice with this simple transformation drill. Do a few examples with the students before you begin, so they know that (with these particular phrasal verbs*) they need to use the verb + pronoun + adverb structure.

* STUDENT SUPPORT For more information on the grammar and use of phrasal verbs, direct the students to Units 128 and 129.

T: Put the message on paper.
SS: Write it down.

T: Cut the trees to the ground.
SS: Cut them down.

T: Reduce the price.
SS: Bring it down.

T: Close the factory completely.
SS: Close it down.

T: Say goodbye to Emma.
SS: See her off.

T: Disconnect the heater.
SS: Switch it off.

T: Connect the kettle.
SS: Switch it on.

T: Try the shoes for size.
SS: Try them on.

T: Extinguish your cigarette.
SS: Put it out.

T: Read the story aloud.
SS: Read it out.

T: Write the list from start to finish.
SS: Write it out.

T: Check your work from start to finish.
SS: Check it over.

T: Increase the prices.
SS: Put them up.

T: Drink all your coffee.
SS: Drink it up.

- Repeat the drill one more time, making sure the students are linking the words as smoothly as possible (e.g. Drink_it_up.)

Exercise C (pairs)
- Put the students in pairs and give them five minutes to do the exercise. Check the answers with the whole class.
- As the students are doing this activity, prepare the board for the next activity.

Extra activity (pairs or small groups)
SPEAKING

- Write these gapped questions on the board or show them on the OHP:

1 Have any shops or cafés closed _____ in your town recently?
2 Do you turn your TV and computer _____ at night, or leave them on standby?
3 Are prices going _____ in your country? Is the price of anything coming _____?
4 Do you always try clothes _____ before you buy them?
5 Do you write _____ example sentences when you learn new grammar and vocabulary?
6 Will you find it easier to work _____ the meanings of new phrasal verbs after this lesson?
7 Have you written _____ all the new phrasal verbs from this lesson?

- Ask the students to call out the correct adverb for each question. [1 down 2 off 3 up, down 4 on 5 out OR down 6 out 7 down]
- Put the students in pairs or small groups to discuss the answers to the questions.
- Invite the groups to report back on their discussions at the end.

Lesson 20 Worksheet

Phrasal verbs – adverb meanings

A Phrasal verbs with **down**

Adverb	**down**			
Meaning	....	**completely to the ground**	....	**on paper**
Example phrasal verbs	turn down the music		the car broke down	

B Phrasal verbs with **off** and **up**

Adverb	**off**		**up**	
Meaning	**away, departing**	....	**increasing**	....
Example phrasal verbs		switch off the heater		eat up those chocolates

C Phrasal verbs with **on** and **over**

Adverb	**on**			**over**
Meaning	**connected**	**wearing**	....	....
Example phrasal verbs			carry on working	check your work over

D Phrasal verbs with **out**

Adverb	**out**			
Meaning	....	**to different people**	....	**from start to finish**
Example phrasal verbs	wash out the dirt		read out the article	

21 Unit 136 Reported requests, offers, etc.

At a glance

1 This lesson focuses on forms of **reported speech** including:
- reported **orders and requests**
- reported **offers and suggestions**.

2 The lesson mainly focuses on **structures with the to-infinitive** (e.g. *He asked to see my ticket. I told her to leave.*) but also includes some **with the -ing form** (e.g. *I suggested going out.*)

3 **Exercises A** and **B** in the book give the students controlled written practice.

4 The **worksheet 'What did she ask? What did he offer?'** provides the students with the opportunity for freer practice of the language input in a communicative context.

Lesson length

45–60 minutes

Preparation

- Copy the people and statements in Demonstration 1 on to the board or an OHT.
- Copy one worksheet for each student in the class.

Demonstration 1

1 Tell the students lots of people spoke to you yesterday. Can they match the people on the left with the statements on the right?

1 A police officer	a She told me to take this medicine.
2 My dentist	b He asked me to turn the music down.
3 My doctor	c He told me not to eat so many sweets.
4 A stranger	d She asked to see my driving licence.
5 My neighbour	e He asked me for some money.

2 Put the students into pairs and give them a minute or two to discuss the answers. Check the answers with the whole class and leave the sentences on the board for Clarification 1. [1d 2c 3a 4e 5b]

Clarification 1

Reported orders and requests (1)

1 The sentences on the board are reported statements and requests. Elicit the direct speech sentences for Sentences a and b, and write them on the board:

	Reported speech	Direct speech
a	She told me to take this medicine.	'You must take this medicine.'
b	He asked me to turn the music down.	'Can you turn the music down?'

2 Ask: *Which of the sentences in direct speech is an order?* [Sentence a.] *What is Sentence b?* [A request.] Highlight the form of the reporting structure:

tell someone to do something (order)
ask someone to do something (request)

3 Elicit the direct speech for Sentence c, and write it on the board:

| | Reported speech | Direct speech |
| c | He told me not to eat so many sweets. | 'Don't eat so many sweets.' |

Highlight the negative form:

ask/tell someone not to do something.

4 Elicit the direct speech for Sentence d, and write it on the board:

| | Reported speech | Direct speech |
| d | She asked to see my driving licence. | 'Can I see your driving licence?' |

We can also use the structure without the object:

ask to do something (but not ~~tell to do something~~)

5 Elicit the direct speech for Sentence e, and write it on the board:

	Reported speech	Direct speech
e	He asked me for some money.	'Can I have some money?'

We use the structure:

ask for something

when someone asks to have something.

Practice 1

Extra activity (whole class)
TRANSFORMATION DRILL

● Give the students some very controlled practice with this transformation drill. Clean the board and ask the students to close their books. How easily can the students transform the direct speech from the clarification back into the reported speech of the demonstration? And can they remember who said each thing?

T: Can I see your driving licence?
SS: A police officer asked to see my driving licence.

T: Can I have some money?
SS: A stranger asked me for some money.

T: Don't eat so many sweets.
SS: My dentist told me not to eat so many sweets.

T: You must take this medicine.
SS: My doctor told me to take this medicine.

T: Can you turn the music down?
SS: My neighbour asked me to turn the music down.

● Repeat the drill a few times until the students are producing the sentences comfortably.

Exercise A (individuals)

● Give the students five minutes to complete Exercise A. Let the students compare answers in pairs before you check the answers with the whole class.

Demonstration 2

1 Write these three sentences on the board:

a I promised to eat fruit, not chocolate.
b I invited him to come to the party.
c I apologized for breaking the speed limit.

Ask: *Who is the speaker addressing in each of these sentences – the police officer, the dentist, the doctor, the stranger or the neighbour?*

Check the answers with the whole class and leave the sentences on the board for Clarification 2. [a the dentist b the neighbour c the police officer]

Clarification 2

Reported offers, suggestions, etc. (2)

1 We can also use certain verb patterns to report other kinds of speech events, such as offers, advice, promises and suggestions. Elicit the direct speech for Sentence a, and write it on the board:

	Reported speech	Direct speech
a	I promised to eat fruit, not chocolate.	'I'll eat fruit, not chocolate – I promise!'

Highlight the form:

verb + to-infinitive.

We can use the verbs **agree, offer, promise, refuse** and **threaten** in this way.

2 Elicit the direct speech for Sentence b, and write it on the board:

Reported speech	Direct speech
I invited him to come to the party.	'Would you like to come to the party?'

Highlight the form:

verb + object + to-infinitive.

We can use the verbs **advise, invite, remind** and **warn** in this way.

3 Elicit the direct speech for Sentence c, and write it on the board:

Reported speech	Direct speech
I apologized for breaking the speed limit.	'I'm sorry I broke the speed limit.'

Highlight the form:

verb + -ing form.

We can use an -ing form after the verbs **admit, apologize for, insist on** and **suggest**.

* STUDENT SUPPORT For more information on the verb patterns see Unit 62 'Verb + to-infinitive or verb + -ing form' and Unit 65 'Verb + object + to-infinitive or -ing form'.

Admit that, insist that, etc. (3)

1 We can use a clause (with **that**) after **admit**, **advise**, **agree**, **insist**, **promise**, **remind**, **suggest** and **warn**. For example:

Trevor admitted (that) he had forgotten the shopping.

You promised (that) you would finish the work by the end of this week.

Note: These structures aren't focused on in this lesson plan. However, if you choose to include this focus in your lesson, Exercise C provides controlled practice.

Practice 2

Exercise B (individuals)

● Give the students five to ten minutes to complete Exercise B. Let the students compare answers in pairs before you check the answers with the whole class.

Exercise B Extension activity (individuals, mingling)
TEST YOUR MEMORY

● Students work in pairs. They look at the speech bubbles in Exercise B but cover the eight sentences (the two examples and Sentences 1–6) below it. They work together to try to remember the eight reported speech sentences.

Extra activity Worksheet (individuals, mingling)
WHAT DID SHE ASK? WHAT DID HE OFFER?

● Give a worksheet to each student in the class. Direct the students to Exercise 1. Give the students five to ten minutes to complete the sentences using their own ideas. (You could do the first one as an example.) Go round the class and check the students' work as they are writing.
● When the students have finished working, get them to move around the class. They should say one of their sentences to another student, then move on and speak to someone else.
● After about five minutes, get the students to sit down again and write down what different people promised, apologized for, suggested, etc.
● To bring the lesson to a close, invite students to read out some of their sentences to the whole class.

Lesson 21 Worksheet

What did she ask? What did he offer?

Speaking

1 Functions. Use the prompts to make requests, offers, etc.

Make a request
Could you .... ?

Make an invitation
Would you like to .... ?

Make a suggestion
Shall we .... ?

Make an apology
I'm sorry I ....

Make an offer
I'll ....

Give a reminder
Don't forget ....

Make a promise
I'll ....

---

2 Move round the class and say your sentences to different students.

Writing

1 Reported functions. Write sentences reporting what people said to you.

_____ asked ....

_____ invited ....

_____ suggested ....

_____ apologized for ....

_____ offered ....

_____ reminded ....

_____ promised ....

At a glance

1 This lesson is a **review of conditionals**. It contrasts:
- **First, Second** and **Third Conditionals**
- **other types of conditional sentence**.

2 **Exercise B** in the book gives controlled written practice of First, Second and Third Conditionals.

3 **Exercise 1** on the **worksheet 'Conditional pairs'** is an adaptation and extension of **Exercise C** in the book, and gives the students further controlled practice including other types of conditional sentence.

4 **Exercise 2** on the **worksheet** provides the opportunity for freer practice.

Lesson length

60 minutes

Preparation

- Photocopy one worksheet for each pair of students. Cut the worksheets in half.

Demonstration

1 Write a title for the lesson on the board:

> Present, past and future possibilities

To set the context, find out who in the class likes football. Have they ever been to see a live football match? Did their team win, lose or draw? How did they feel?

2 Give the students a few minutes to look at the people in the pictures at the top of page 352 and to read what they are saying. Ask: *Did their team win?* [No.]

Tell the students to look at the speech bubbles. Ask: *Which sentence is about the past? Which is about the future? Which is about the present?* Write the sentences clearly on the board in readiness for Clarification 1.

> Present possibility: If he (Johnson) was in the team, I'd feel more confident.
> Future possibility: If we win today, we'll go to the top of the league.
> Past possibility: If Johnson had played, we'd have won.

Clarification 1

First, Second and Third Conditionals (1)

1 There are three main types of conditional.

* STUDENT SUPPORT This lesson assumes some knowledge of the three main types. For more information on the First, Second and Third Conditionals, direct the students to Units 144, 145 and 146.

Highlight the form of the 'future possibility' sentence on the board:

> **If** + Present Simple **will**
> If we <u>win</u> today,   we'<u>ll</u> go to the top of the league.

Ask: *Is the first future event certain?* [No. We might win. It's a possible future event.] *Is the future consequence of the event certain?* [Yes. Winning = going to the top of the league.]

Ask: *What kind of conditional is this?* [The First Conditional.]

If the first event is <u>certain</u> to lead to the second event, we use **will**. If the second event is also only a possibility, we can also use other modals such as **might** and **can**. For example: *If we win today, I <u>might</u> buy you dinner.*

2 Focus on the 'present possibility' sentence on the board. Ask: *Is Johnson in the team today?* [No – this sentence is imagining a different version of the present.] Highlight the form:

> **If** + Past Simple   **would**
> If Johnson <u>was</u> in the team,   I'<u>d</u> feel more confident.

Ask: *What kind of conditional is this?* [The Second Conditional.]

Other modal verbs can also be used with the Second Conditional. For example: *If Johnson <u>was</u> in the team, I <u>could</u> relax a bit.*

3 Focus on the 'past possibility' sentence on the board. Ask: *Did Johnson play in the team?* [No – this sentence is imagining a different version of the past.] Highlight the form:

If + Past Perfect	would + have + past participle
If Johnson <u>had played</u>,	we'<u>d have won</u>.

Ask: *What kind of conditional is this?* [The Third Conditional.]

Other modal verbs can also be used with the Third Conditional. For example: *If Johnson had played, we might have won.*

Practice 1

Exercise B (individuals, pairs)

- Tell the class they are going to read a conversation between a music student called Adam and his landlord (the man Adam rents a room from), Mr Day. Write these three questions on the board:

  > 1 What musical instrument does Adam play?
  > 2 Why is Mr Day unhappy?
  > 3 What might Mr Day do?

- Give the students one minute to read the conversation quickly and answer the questions. Check the correct answers with the whole class. [1 The trumpet. 2 Adam practises the trumpet at night. 3 Complain to Adam's college.]
- Give the students a few minutes to complete Exercise B. Let them compare their answers in pairs, then check the correct answers with the whole class.
- Put the students in pairs to practise reading the conversation.

  Exercise B Extension activity (whole class)
  TRANSFORMATION DRILL

- Use this transformation drill to give the students practice using **might** (**not**) in conditional sentences. Tell the students they need to make each of your sentences sound less certain by using **might / might not** instead of **would / wouldn't** and **will / won't**.

  T: If I don't practice, I **won't** pass my exam.
  SS: If I don't practice, I **might not** pass my exam.

  T: If you had told me about this trumpet when you first came here, I **wouldn't** have let you have the room.
  SS: If you had told me about this trumpet when you first came here, I **might not** have let you have the room.

T: If you didn't play so loud, it **wouldn't** be so bad.
SS: If you didn't play so loud, it **might not** be so bad.

T: If you go on making this noise at night, I'll have to complain to your college.
SS: If you go on making this noise at night, I **might** have to complain to your college.

- Go through the drill a few times until the students can produce sentences comfortably.
  Note: These are long sentences, so allow the students some time to think about and produce each one.

Clarification 2

Other conditional sentences (2)

1 As well as the three main types, there are other types of conditional sentences. Write this sentence on the board:

> If you ring this number, no one answers.

Ask: *Is this sentence about a present possibility or a present fact?* [A present fact. The second event, 'no one answers', always happens as a result of the first event, 'you ring this number'.] Highlight the form:

If + Present Simple	Present Simple
If you <u>ring</u> this number,	no one <u>answers</u>.

This structure is called the Zero Conditional.

* STUDENT SUPPORT For more information on the Zero Conditional, direct the students to Unit 144.4.

2 We can also use a present-tense verb and an imperative. For example: *If you <u>need</u> any help, just <u>ask</u>. If <u>you're thinking</u> of watching the football tonight, <u>don't bother</u>.*

Ask the class: *Are these sentences similar to the Zero Conditional or the First Conditional?* [The First Conditional. The sentences are about future possibilities.]

3 We can use **be going to** in conditional sentences. It is often used instead of **will**. For example: *If they don't give me a refund, I'<u>m going to</u> complain.*

It can also be used in the **if** clause: *If it'<u>s going to</u> rain, I'd better take an umbrella.*

4 We can mix the Second and Third Conditionals. For example: *If our team <u>had won</u>, I <u>wouldn't be</u> in such a bad mood now.*

* STUDENT SUPPORT For more information on mixing the Second and Third Conditionals, direct the students to Unit 146.4.

Practice 2

Worksheet (pairs)

CONDITIONAL PAIRS – EXERCISE 1

- This exercise is an extension of Exercise C in the book. Before you begin, write the example question on the board:

> You think Emma should book a seat on the train. The alternative is having to stand.

- Ask the whole class to transform it into one sentence beginning with **If**.
- Write the answer on the board:

> If Emma doesn't book a seat on the train, she'll have to stand.

- Divide the class into two groups, Group A and Group B. Give a Student A worksheet to all the students in Group A, and a Student B worksheet to all the students in Group B. Give the students five to ten minutes to transform the six sentences on their worksheet into different kinds of conditional sentences beginning with **If**. Students can work in AA and BB pairs at this stage.
- Reorganize the class into AB pairs to check their answers with each other. Student A has the answers for Student B on his/her worksheet, and vice versa. As the students check their answers, they will notice that they have parallel conditional sentences on their worksheets. When all the pairs have finished checking their answers, check with the class what types of conditionals Sentences 1 to 6 are. Do the example sentence with the whole class: *If Emma doesn't book a seat on the train, she'll have to stand.* = First Conditional. [1 Third Conditional. 2 First Conditional. 3 Second Conditional. 4 mixed Third and Second Conditionals. 5 First Conditional, with imperative. 6 Zero Conditional.]

Extra activity Worksheet (pairs)

CONDITIONAL PAIRS – EXERCISE 2

- Students can continue working in the same AB pairs for this activity. Direct students to Exercise 2 on the worksheet. Give them about ten minutes to complete the next six sentences by adding their own ideas to those given on the worksheet. Their six sentences should follow the same six conditional types as seen in Exercise 1 on the worksheet.
- Reorganize the students back into the original two groups, Group A and Group B. Give them a few minutes to read out and compare their sentences.

- To bring the lesson to a close, invite the students to read out their funniest or most inventive conditional sentences.

Exercise A

- Exercise A could be set for homework.

Lesson 22 Worksheet

Conditional pairs

Student A

1 What might you say in these situations? Use a conditional sentence.

You think Emma should book a seat on the train. The alternative is having to stand.
If Emma doesn't book a seat on the train, she'll have to stand.

1 You didn't know how unpopular Jason was when you invited him to your party.
If...

2 Warn your friend not to put too many tins into the plastic bag or it'll break.
If...

3 You haven't got a pen, so you can't write down the address.
If...

4 You should have started your project earlier. You're so far behind now.
If...

5 Your friend might need some help. If so, tell her to give you a ring.
If...

6 The automatic result of the door opening is the fan coming on.
If...

Answers for Student B
1 If I'd known how nice Ella was, I would have spoken to her earlier.
2 If you put too many books on to that shelf, it'll fall down.
3 If I knew the answer, I would tell you.
4 If I hadn't gone to bed so late last night, I wouldn't feel so sleepy now.
5 If the phone rings tonight, don't answer it.
6 If you cook nuts for more than a few minutes, they burn.

---

2 Write six more conditional sentences that follow the same patterns as the sentences in the exercise above.

1 If I had known...

2 If you put...

3 If I had a / an..

4 If..,
I wouldn't feel so awful today.

5 If..,
don't worry about it.

6 If..,
it's very painful!

Lesson 22 Worksheet

Conditional pairs

Student B

1 What might you say in these situations? Use a conditional sentence.

You think Emma should book a seat on the train. The alternative is having to stand.
If Emma doesn't book a seat on the train, she'll have to stand.

1 You didn't know how nice Ella was. That's why you didn't speak to her earlier.
If...

2 Warn your friend not to put too many books on to the shelf or it'll fall down.
If...

3 You don't know the answer so you can't tell your friend.
If...

4 You shouldn't have gone to bed so late last night. You feel so sleepy now.
If...

5 The phone might ring tonight. Tell your friend not to answer it.
If...

6 The result of cooking nuts for more than a few minutes is that they burn.
If...

Answers for Student A
1 If I'd known how unpopular Jason was, I wouldn't have invited him to my party.
2 If you put too many tins into the plastic bag, it'll break.
3 If I had a pen, I could write down the address.
4 If I had started my project earlier, I wouldn't be so far behind now.
5 If you need some help, give me a ring.
6 If you open the door, the fan comes on.

---

2 Write six more conditional sentences that follow the same patterns as the sentences in the exercise above.

1 If I had known...

2 If you put...

3 If I had a / an..

4 If..,
I wouldn't feel so awful today.

5 If..,
don't worry about it.

6 If..,
it's very painful!